Isabelle's Dream

Madeleine Herrmann

Plain View Press
http://plainviewpress.net

3800 N. Lamar, Suite 730-260
Austin, TX 78756

Copyright © 2012 **Madeleine Herrmann.** All rights reserved under International and Pan-American Copyright Conventions. No part of this book may be reproduced or distributed in any form or by any means, or stored in a data base or retrieval system, without written permission from the author. All rights, including electronic, are reserved by the author and publisher.

ISBN: 978-1-935514-21-3
Library of Congress Control Number: 2012950151

Cover art: Family photo of Aunt Marraine.
        Photo replication courtesy of Thomas French
Cover design by Pam Knight

Acknowledgments

I acknowledge and thank the people who have encouraged me to take dreams seriously and to look into them with questions about my life: My aunt Marraine when I was a little girl, Anne Langford, my professor at JFK University, Pat Sargent's enlightened dream group in Taos, and my dear son Steven Herrmann, a Jungian psychotherapist. They all helped me see the importance of dreams and to write this story.

More recently I have been helped by the friends who read the manuscript and commented on it: Kathy Mayes from Austin, Josette Hurwitz from Tucson, Suzanne Brock from Taos and finally my wonderful writing coach Cinny Green from Santa Fe, who also edited the story with understanding and advice.

I also thank my partner and loving supporter Thomas French who is always there to encourage me in difficult times.

This story is dedicated to the memory of my dear Aunt Marraine, who was my godmother and role model when I was growing up. I did not realize how important she had been in my life until I got older and saw how she contributed to who I became as a woman. In *Isabelle's Dream* she appears in essence as the character Justine. Thank you, Marraine, for teaching me what true beauty really is.

Contents

The Dream		7
I	The Meadow	9
II	The Stream	29
III	The Women	39
IV	The Forest	63
V	Grandmother	73
VI	The Spider Web	83
VII	The Ermine Scarf	97
VIII	The Smile	111
IX	White Lace	129
X	The Kick	137
XI	The Mirror	145
XII	Long Black Dresses	149
XIII	Snakes	157
XIV	A Woman Named Isabelle	163
About the Author		169

The Dream

She was walking in a meadow with her mother. It was a large meadow, a clearing in the middle of a pine forest. Wildflowers grew amidst the tall grasses and a small stream ran near a long line of trees. Sunlight spread through the spider webs stretched between branches. There was an old-fashioned mirror standing right in the middle of the meadow, an oval shape, which could flip around in its mahogany stand when touched. Intrigued, Isabelle cautiously walked to it, as if drawn by an unknown force. She stopped close to it and stood for a while with her eyes closed, and then resolutely forced her eyes open and looked at herself in the mirror. She was smiling.

Isabelle also noticed the reflection of a group of women standing near the trees behind her, poised like an old formal photograph. She turned. It was her grandmother and her grand aunt, Justine, among a few others dressed in long black dresses and white lace shawls. She ran toward them, her arms wide open, but they vanished in the sunlit mist. Puzzled, Isabelle looked back at her mother, who was just entering the meadow. Together they walked to the center of the field near the mirror where an old furry scarf lay crumpled on the ground. A dead snake lay in front of it. Her mother kicked it, to see whether it was still alive. Isabelle said, "Be careful, it's a cottonmouth, a dangerous snake. See its fangs."

"I was wondering where this was," said her mother, and she reached down for the scarf. As her hand grasped it, the snake came alive and stood straight up, black and fierce…

1

The Meadow

Isabelle woke up, gasping aloud, terrified. Her startled cat jumped down from its nest on the comforter and ran under the bed. Isabelle sat up, breathing deeply, trying to calm herself. A pale early May light filtered through the window shade. "Too early to get up," she thought, as she snuggled back under the covers, still shaking. Jasmine nudged her purring nose into Isabelle's cheeks, and then reassured, the cat curled back into its favorite spot.

Isabelle couldn't get back to sleep, though. Too many things ran through her head. Her mother, the scarf, the snake, the relatives… and suddenly she wished George were there. George was always sweet when she was ready to go to sleep, putting his loving arms around her. She missed him. She missed him a lot.

She rolled on her back and clutched the covers up to her neck. Would she ever be free of the ongoing tape spinning through her head since she had separated from George three months ago? Did I do the right thing? Will I ever find another man to love me? Where is my strange life headed? She had just turned fifty in March, and there had been something weighing on her ever since. George was only part of it. It was at the same time an urge and a fear which she fought back by using tried-and-true mental tricks, by substituting the negative with thoughts of nature, thoughts of elegant colors, inspiring scenes from books, and melodies of classical music but mostly she kept herself distracted by her very busy schedule of school events, movies, outings with friends, and trips to her widowed mother's house in the Gold Country. A tight agenda made her feel secure and put boundaries around the ongoing dialogue with herself. When she was overcome with upsetting thoughts, she looked at them—or avoided them—in the reassuring framework of her duties.

Isabelle sighed. Her life wasn't really so bad. She liked to teach French and her two-bedroom condo was easy to care for. She had no obligations she didn't choose, no children to look after, no particular plans for summer vacation, and her plan for the weekend was today's lovely drive to her mother's antique shop in Mokelumne Hill. A completely free summer vacation lay a month ahead.

Her mother, Marguerite, had been in her dream, she recalled, along with the odd tableau of her relatives. Isabelle looked at the clock. 5:30 was too early to call and ask her what she thought of the snake and the scarf and the old women in black satin and lace. Well, she could tell her later. Deciding to get up and pack, Isabelle slipped her feet over the edge of the bed, but she immediately dropped her lean body back on the comforter. Roused again, Jasmine complained loudly. "Oh, hush, cat," Isabelle scolded. "I can't sleep but I can't get up, either."

It simply wouldn't take Isabelle very long to pack for a night away. Her bag was ready at a moment's notice to fill with toiletries and a few clothes. Swift and efficient packing became a habit after George moved in with her a few years before. She had learned to be ready on the spot when, on any Friday, he might arrive home after work announcing: "Guess where we're going today?"

There was a magic moment after this question, an alluring sense of expectation, a picture painted in her wild imagination. She became filled with thoughts of adventure, of love making, of delicious foods and beautiful surroundings, of all the good things that make life exciting. Enchanted, she'd hug him and say, "I can't imagine where."

George always chose someplace lovely: Carmel, the Sonoma Valley, Tomales Bay, the Russian River, Lake Tahoe, Yosemite Park—any place they could reach within a few hours drive from the San Francisco Bay area. As a real estate agent, he knew them all well. They would stay in bed-and-breakfast inns, take walks, eat in bistros, make love, and sleep late. Exotic days and erotic nights—for the first couple of years.

Isabelle pressed her palms against her eyes trying not to remember the day she'd kicked him out. But the memory leapt into her mind like a child hiding in a corner then jumping out with a loud Boo! After a few months, George's magic wore off as his business plummeted with the real estate crash. The romantic get-a-ways became unimaginative shortcuts of previous trips with many stops at local bars along the way. She often had to drive because George became dangerously giddy and overconfident. That last night she had smelled liquor on his breath as soon as he walked in the door with the familiar words, now less inviting and more imperative: "Pack up. Let's go." Less than ten miles down the highway, he pulled her Camry into the parking lot of a tavern along the highway. She pleaded, "George, don't stop yet. Let's keep going so we can walk on the beach tonight."

"Shit, that bastard took the best parking space."

"We can stay in the little red cabana under the trees."

He opened his door and shivered. "California is supposed to be so perfect but here I am, cold as a codfish. C'mon, Isabelle. Move it. I gotta get inside."

She put her hand on his arm. "George, please. Not tonight."

He mimicked her. "Not tonight, George."

"Why are you drinking so much? I think you need to take a break. Tell me what's going on. I know business is hard… "

"What are you, my mother?" he sneered. "Well, wait in the car, Mommy. But I'm getting bourbon."

He staggered to the front door of the bar, and when he pulled it open, Isabelle could hear the tin can sound of a country jukebox and smell the stale beer. They never got any closer to the beach. As she sat next to him at the bar breathing in acrid second-hand cigarette smoke, George got into a loud argument with a construction worker about President George Bush as he downed four drinks in a row. The bartender finally escorted the staggering George to the car, and Isabelle drove them back to her condo where he fell onto the couch and clunked into the heavy, snorting sleep of the inebriated. Isabelle stood over him for a minute. Foolishly, she had kept hoping the downward pattern would change without believing, deep down, that it really would. She now realized she'd hung on to the good parts with Pollyanna-ish optimism—another week, another day because he loved her, didn't he?

When she awoke early that bleak Saturday morning in January, she walked downstairs smelling his sour clothes strewn over the furniture and saw another broken bottle on the kitchen floor. Enough. If this was love, she wanted no more of it. She yanked the covers off his pale body, once athletic but now bloated and white like a beached fish. "Get out, George. Now," she stated, surprised at the way her voice sounded determined and calm when her insides were churning.

"Leave me alone," he mumbled from under a sofa pillow. "I'm sick."

"You're hung over and I told you I can't take it anymore. This is my place and you have to leave."

George slowly pulled the pillow off his face. His eyes were red and his beard dotted with pretzel crumbs. "Wait a minute. Honey, we can… "

"No. I'll go out and get my coffee. When I get back, I want you gone. Everything. Clothes and all. Go and don't call." She felt a sob clutch her throat at the look of shock in his face, but she swallowed it. He looked baffled and lost, so she turned before the rush to comfort him crumbled her resolve. She ran down the stairs to the parking lot and drove to the local Starbucks where she buried her face in a newspaper and consoled herself with a latte. When she returned to the condo an hour later, he was gone, and she hadn't heard from him since. Yet that cajoling look still haunted her.

When she looked at the clock again, she was glad to see an hour had passed even though it had been another hour of obsessive memories. She got up and first put enough food and water in Jasmine's large bowls to last well until her return on Sunday evening, watered her pink azalea, her white begonia, and her ficus. She closed a couple blinds on the south side and then packed her small blue overnight bag. By mid morning she was ready to head to the country. The irony of loading her bag on the back seat of the Camry, as she had so often done before, caught up with her. "Here I am, escaping again. Something is making me run." Isabelle looked in the rearview mirror at trees that lined the driveway and remembered her dream, half expecting the staid old relatives to poke their faces around the trunks. She backed out and headed toward Highway 4 with a puzzled smile on her face.

ISABELLE SETTLED INTO the two-hour drive to Mokelumne Hill. Her body slumped behind the wheel, pulled into the seat by sadness. She had taken the drive many times since her mother had moved there a few years before, so she knew every little town on the way, every railroad crossing, and freeway overpass. She could navigate without looking at a map or road sign, and to cheer herself up, she decided to stop at a few favorite spots.

An hour from Stockton, she stopped at the Oak Ridge Winery in Lodi and bought her mother a bottle of chardonnay. Set between the Sierra Nevada foothills and San Francisco Bay, Lodi's warm days and cool evening breezes from the sea created a Mediterranean climate for grape cultivation. She and Marguerite always went to the Lodi Grape Festival in the fall for a day of wine tasting. The vineyards and the wine inspired her normally taciturn mother to reminisce about growing up in southern France.

Last fall, while they walked through the winery's famous barrel-shaped tasting room, Marguerite had said, "These hardwood floors smell just like the ones in my parents' house, like fresh wax. The dark wood made everyone quiet and so well mannered. A bit stiff and solemn compared to Americans, though."

Isabelle tasted a rich Zinfandel. "But your French cooking isn't solemn, Mother. This would go well with your roast beef."

Marguerite took a little sip. "You mean the one with mustard butter sauce? Yes, it would."

They walked to the table with white wines. "It was amazing what miracles your grandmother Mamie created in our kitchen, though." Marguerite sniffed an Oak Ridge Chardonnay and twirled it in the glass. "Herbs sat in little pots on the windowsill. Gorgeous copper pots glittered in the dim light."

"I don't feel very French anymore, even though I'm fluent enough in the language to teach it." Isabelle sighed.

Marguerite laughed. "The only thing that made my parents madder than my marrying a resistance fighter during the war was marrying an American after the war." She paused and tilted her head. "And taking their only grandchild to the States."

Isabelle and Marguerite grew quiet as each remembered the dashing David Chalmers in her own way. Isabelle never met her own father, the resistance hero who was killed in 1945 just before she was born, but David had been a wonderful parent and she missed him very much. He had died of a heart attack ten years ago. Alive and vital one day, gone the next. Marguerite mourned deeply and quietly. She wouldn't discuss her grief but it emanated from the dark caves of her brown eyes every time Isabelle visited. Yet, a year after David's death, Isabelle showed up at her mother's townhouse in San Francisco and found Marguerite signing papers with a real estate agent.

Isabelle was stunned. "Did you buy some property, Mother?"

Marguerite nodded once. The California-blond agent raised her hands in joy. "Your mother just purchased a treasure, an absolute treasure: an historical building in Mokelumne Hill."

Isabelle grimaced. "What kind of name is that?"

Marguerite waved away her daughter's tone. "Actually it was one of the richest gold-mining towns in California." She looked down at the realtor's flyer. "It says: 'Mokelumne Hill took its name from the river, which was named after a Mi-wok Indian village. The Indians were locally known as the Mokels, and the Mi-wok suffix *umne* means 'people of.' How charming. People of Mi-wok. That'll be a good story to tell my customers."

"Customers?"

"I've been up there twice now. Because of its history and the local restored hotel, it gets lots of tourists and hikers and bicyclists. I'll be able to walk into the mountains from my back door."

The realtor closed her briefcase with a satisfied snap and reached out to hand Marguerite a set of keys. "My dear, I wish you all the best with your antique shop." The woman turned and her high heels tapped loudly across the tile floor as she headed out the door.

Shocked, Isabelle had asked, "An antique store? I didn't know you… "

Marguerite held up two hands, palms out. "This is what I've always wanted to do. I went from being a child to being a wife—two times—and then motherhood. I need to be self-sufficient. As my father would say, *L'heure c'est l'heure*. I will run my own business."

"THE HOUR IS the hour. It's time!" Isabelle said aloud as she drove away from the winery's tasting room where she and her mother had sipped wines. She laughed at the memory. Marguerite had used that phrase her whole life to get Isabelle out of bed, to school, to activities, and everything else. It left no room for argument. On to the antique shop!

Isabelle drove higher into the hills listening to Mozart's Piano Concerto in E-Major. Near Sutter Creek she paused at the magical Daffodil Hills, a private park with a spectacle of yellow and white blossoms, set against a background of flowering trees in bright and tender pink. Walking through gardens of 300,000 daffodils was a marvel to her. The four acres of flowers were not a business; no one sold any of the flowers. It was a family's seasonal gift to all who stopped along the road.

Isabelle breathed in the scent of loam and greenery. She heard the fields whisper, "Spring is here, and spring is boundless." It's a spell, as if I am becoming spring for a while, she mused as she walked the groomed paths through the blossoms. She sensed David walking beside her because they had come here together every year when she was a child. He brought a camera and would lie on his belly to get close-ups of the blossoms. Isabelle would climb all over him as he protested with mock sternness, "Get off me, you monkey!" Then he would carry her on his shoulders or she'd run ahead in bursts of joy. The only time he had gotten angry with her was when she ran off the path, lay down in the blossoms, and looked up through the shimmering yellow and white petals. The colors had merged in her iris, and her child's body had felt in harmony with the plants swaying above and around her. The moment only lasted a minute until David called sharply, "No, Isabelle. Get back on the path right now." His tone couldn't alter the inexorable connection, though. She had broken the rules, crushed some flowers, and gotten seriously reprimanded, but her transgression forever engaged her in the profound intricacies of nature. She watched the elements around her differently from then on and sought out places untouched by humans or gently nourished, like Daffodil Hills. She loved the faithfulness and resilience of the natural world, the ever-changing settings and attire.

Nature was always there for her, a silent friend, strong and comforting, a stable confidante, a haven full of soothing surprises.

When she came upon a redwood bench under a pine, Isabelle also remembered she had been here the year before with George at her side. Had she been happier then, she wondered? Not really. They had been going to see Mother, who was not very fond of George. He knew it and was petulantly disengaged, complaining about his back and the sun and anything to call attention to himself and intrude upon the meditative mood of the gardens. He had sat on this bench and refused to walk another step, so of course, they returned to the car.

She didn't feel happier today either, she decided. Her emotions were too entwined in loss and confusion about what to do next, but the daffodils were nature's universal message of awakening, beauty, and promise. An emotion of renewal brought a warm flush to her face. And she could feel it, like the bubbling laughter that burst from her as she wrestled with David, her father. Isabelle put her hand on her chest, feeling spring inside her as well as around her.

This moment was a strictly private affair between herself and the surrounding elements, independent of the presence of any man. Funny how I am! Isabelle thought, I haven't had that many lovers—maybe four or five—but they all made life rain or shine for me, and I withered in the rain. I did not know how to protect myself from it. I guess I got all wet. I can accept anything from nature and even find great comfort in a rainy day. Why can't I love a man that way?

Isabelle left Daffodil Hill returning to Highway 49. She opened her window and let the air rush through the car. Driving on alone now gave her a sense of power. She could do exactly what she wanted in the moment: speed up, look at the landscape, stop, sing, scream, think back, think ahead, say things aloud in this small contained safe space of hers, things she usually did not dare to express, even to herself. Furthermore, she could let her imagination take flight and become someone else driving the purring machine. So one minute she was a woman pioneer driving west in a covered wagon. The next turn in the road she became a pretty young woman going to meet her secret lover in a mountain retreat. Not to indulge in too much silly romanticism she imagined herself as a disgruntled housewife covering her tracks, while running away from her husband to an undisclosed haven. In this protected environment of her moving car, Isabelle could be and do anything.

Isabelle started to chant random syllables emanating deep from her chest, and she let the rhythm of the sounds become a poem straight out of her heart, the non-words were romantic love that always had refused to materialize for her. Next she chanted as if she were reciting a nursery rhyme. On and on down the highway Isabelle chanted loudly, shamelessly, lovingly, hopefully, she chanted her ideals and her dreams until only a dry throat quieted her voice.

The road followed the Sierra foothills, winding through their magnificent spring bounty of variegated greens. The whole scene, under an unbounded blue sky, radiated enough liveliness to inspire the most depressed soul. Isabelle dropped a Beethoven sonata into the tape player, turned the volume up high and bathed in the inspiring music. She stepped on the gas and drove with one hand, tapping the scherzo with her fingers in a happy rapture, when she saw some flashing lights in her rear view mirror.

The policeman in mirror sunglasses walked slowly up to the car when she pulled over. He leaned toward her open window. "Lady, did you know you have been going eighty miles an hour for the past two miles?"

"No Officer, I didn't. I'm sorry. I never got a speeding ticket before. You can check. Here's my license."

He looked over every detail on her license in an unbearable silence, which Isabelle finally had to break. "Officer, I have a very important question to ask you, "Are you a rain or a shine man?" She smiled at her own joke. "This could make a lot of difference, you know."

The policeman never flinched, never acknowledged her question much less answered it. He took her license back to his squad car and spent twenty minutes writing her speeding ticket. He handed it to her just as the sonata ended.

IT WAS LATE AFTERNOON when Isabelle arrived at her mother's store in Mokelumne Hill. As soon as she stepped out of the car, she could smell Marguerite's traditional rabbit stew cooking in the little kitchen of the apartment in back of the antique shop. She wondered how the customers responded to this added feature when they browsed about. It probably helped sales. Her mother was an excellent French cook. Isabelle had been brought up on slowly simmered delicacies, fresh fruits and vegetables purchased daily, heavenly pastries and breads, all the very best that cooking has to offer and this, long before the average American had even discovered the baguette, croissant, or Dijon mustard.

Isabelle's Dream

Isabelle walked through the store, holding her bag close to her body in order to avoid bumping into the many treasures that filled the fragrant space. Marguerite's fantasy had become a reality. She had been able to pull together all of her hidden resources and talent to make a success of the small shop, although Isabelle guessed that her mother's adjustment was not always easy. Sometimes Marguerite would call several times a week—just to talk—but her tone of voice was a bit tight. Isabelle asked if she was alright and her mother always said, "But of course." The antique shop had thrived under her attentive eye and was now such a delight for her that interestingly, now in her seventies, Marguerite had become the one whom Isabelle would visit often—just to talk—and find solace in her mother's presence.

She took a deep breath. There had to be red wine in the stew, and bay leaves and onions, for sure. She just knew it! A couple customers were lost behind a huge vestry cabinet, discussing its merits and age. Another carefully examined a pile of china dishes displayed in an old case against the wall, taking them out one by one. There was a section of gold mining equipment with pans and scales, old books and maps from the 49ers time, tin dishes and goblets. There was a small locked case that had a few precious nuggets in it. Close to the entrance and displayed in the show window were porcelain dolls, smiling enigmatically, in their surroundings of linens and lace, and an old fashioned rocking cradle with a "Fragile, Do Not Touch" sign on it. Some estate jewelry was lit by a blue Tiffany lamp on the top of a cedar chest next to a Louis Vuitton cabin trunk that probably traveled with a wealthy ship passenger a century ago. An Indian section displayed rugs, jewelry, pottery, a few colorful feathers, and heishi beads. And then, there was all of that furniture lining the walls or standing next to each other to form narrow alleys: restored beds and tired Singer sewing machines, a couple of armoires from the old country, including the one from Marguerite's parents, which she had brought along on one of her trips, three roll-top desks, a Murphy bed, several ice boxes and two well seasoned pot belly stoves, all of these items carefully filled or covered with old revues, newspapers, yellowed post cards written in careful scripts, coin collections, and small trinkets of all kinds. Against the back brick wall, two neon signs flashed "Coca-Cola" and "Chevrolet" on a poorly lit section of the store. In the front was a shiny brass cash register in good working order that added a nostalgic metallic ring of gone-by days to the still scene set by the other silent witnesses to history. In this small universe, time had stopped long ago.

Isabelle walked through the wide-open cast iron double door that separated the store from her mother's apartment. She walked in and surprised Marguerite, a wooden spoon on her tongue, tasting the stew.

After they kissed on each cheek, Isabelle said, "Mother, this place is getting more cluttered every time I visit you!" She added with a grin, "How can you stand all that junk?"

"You don't know anything about antiques Isabelle, so be quiet. You should see what I bought the other day at the auction in Auburn! The most incredible wooden horse you have ever seen. Look!"

In a corner of the tiny living room, adjacent to the kitchen, Isabelle's eyes fell upon an old small wooden horse right out of a fairy tale, so light and sweet looking. It smiled as if to invite her to hop on a merry-go-round. The bright colors on its body had softened with time but the gilded mane still flowed lavishly.

"It is so beautiful. Are you really going to sell it?"

"I don't know yet. Anyway, here you are Isabelle. Just in time for dinner," Marguerite grinned back at her with the same impish look, "as usual."

"I knew you were cooking *un civet de lapin* the minute I walked in."

"My customers love it. Yesterday a woman asked for my recipe to make a French apple pie I was baking. There is some of it for dessert tonight. Go get yourself settled. I am just going to lock up now and we'll have a quiet evening."

Isabelle put her bag down next to the couch—which would later be opened into a bed for her—and walked into the bathroom to refresh herself. A superb Victorian stained-glass window rested on the West side of the room, filtering the sunset through fragments of purple and deep pink flowers with a hint of green and grey in the background. There were other stained glass windows in the small apartment, but this one was her very favorite. Isabelle did not like antiques, particularly, but some of her mother's treasures, she had to admit, were absolutely lovely.

"That's it," Marguerite called a few minutes later from the living room, "store's closed for today. That last customer bought a couple of my china plates and another one, this morning, fell in love with my oldest doll—the one with the long baptismal satin dress and an angelic face. You know the one? He said he would be back tomorrow to get it. I sure hope so. Business has been very slow lately." Marguerite sighed and brushed a curl of hair away from her face. "I hate it when it's like that; there isn't much to do."

"Except cook for your daughter and make her happy and fat. I'm here to give you something to fill your time, and you know I love your cooking. I bought some chardonnay from the Oak Ridge Winery. Remember how crisp it is?"

"Hail to California, the land of plenty—especially wine."

"So, you think that you might not sell the little wooden horse, mother? Could you consider keeping it for me? Anyway, there are some other things in the store I think you shouldn't sell."

"Like what?"

"Like this marvelous armoire you brought from your parents' house. It has so much sentimental value. Why would you want to get rid of it?"

"Did you look at the price tag?"

"Yes. $5500."

"Way over priced. I just put it there with an unrealistic price tag because I didn't have room for it in the apartment. But if I sell it, it could pay for a lavish wedding reception for you… "

"Mother, it's not funny. You know I just broke up with George."

Marguerite shrugged. "*Tant pis*. Too bad… maybe. But I am glad that you like the little wooden horse. I thought that you might, so it is all yours, *chérie*, and you can take it with you."

Isabelle hugged her mother. Marguerite laughed. "Sit, sit, before you make me spill."

She ladled stew into two bowls and set them on the table with a baguette and fresh green salad. All through dinner, the mother and daughter, now friends, continued their kidding exchange, teasing each other in a duel of carefully chosen phrases, laughing, raising their voices or their arms, imitating each other in jest with a plain warm expression of love floating about the room.

After dinner, Marguerite retired to her small bedroom saying, "Sleep well, Isabelle. Enjoy a silent night in the Gold Country." Isabelle pulled open the sofa bed and nestled under a French down comforter, but it took her a while to get to sleep. At first, it was pitch dark outside. As her mother had predicted, the night became very still, except for a few dogs barking now and then. Behind the heavy cast iron doors, now closed, Isabelle visualized the store, with its parade of relics from the past fidgeting in their ghostly slumber. Slowly a timid crescent moon rose behind a blue iris stained glass window near the sofa bed. "If only I could understand the waves emanating from these antiques. If things could only speak," she murmured as she dozed off, "but the White Lace past is an eternal mystery."

WHEN ISABELLE WOKE UP, she felt refreshed and lighthearted. In the tiny kitchen, Marguerite had started brewing the coffee and was about to take a batch of croissants out of the oven. When she was a child, an aromatic home cooked meal or a savory treat had always softened any hardship Isabelle felt. Marguerite never coddled her daughter but food was her way to speak her love.

"Come and have breakfast, sleepy head. It is already eight, and I'll have to open the store very soon. Actually, we'll have some time together today. I asked my friend Naomi to work for me for a few hours. She loves to work here. She's retired and has so much free time she doesn't know what to do with it. She doesn't even want to get paid but I make her take a commission on her sales. It's great for me. She gives me more freedom to go hunting for treasures and she's fun to work with."

"Mother, you've always had terrific friends. How do you do it?"

"Well, maybe it's my superb cooking, but more probably, my sweet personality."

"Ah, so humble."

"What's that 'Ah'?" Marguerite grinned and handed her daughter a cup of café au lait.

Isabelle took it with an impish nod of thanks and walked to the bathroom while her mother set the breakfast table. She splashed some cold water on her face, then dried it while looking at herself in the full-length mirror on the back of the door. She remembered her smile in the dream she'd had the night before. Maybe she had something to smile about after all. She liked her slim body, rendered athletic by her steady workouts at the spa. She examined her face, running her fingers over her slightly prominent French nose and blinking her warm brown eyes. I'm rather good looking, she admitted silently. Vivacious and soft at the same time. She turned her head to the side. Her dark hair was turning grey, there were a few expressive lines around her eyes and her mouth, but on the whole, her appearance was fairly youthful. Isabelle liked the image the mirror reflected back to her and she smiled again, shaking her head at her girlish preoccupation with her appearance.

"Are you coming, Isabelle?" called Marguerite. "The croissants are on the table."

Isabelle joined her in the kitchen, and there were not only croissants on the table, but strawberries with cream, fresh apple juice, homemade jams, and a pot of great smelling coffee.

"Did you sleep well?"

Isabelle poured herself another cup of coffee and served them both a croissant. "Much better than the night before."

"Were you worrying about something?"

Isabelle paused. "It's a general state of mind the last month or so. Like an imperceptible shift in a fault line. Underground but disturbing."

"I'm not sure I understand."

"How to explain? Well, I had a startling dream that woke me up. You and I were in a meadow looking at an antique mirror. You know the standing kind on a swivel?"

"Oval?"

"Yes, exactly. I saw the reflection of our old French relatives, including Mamie."

"Oh dear, was she scolding us?"

"They seemed oddly stern but inviting. Then we saw an old furry scarf on the ground near a dead snake. Only of course, the snake wasn't dead at all. That's when I woke up."

Marguerite shivered. "I absolutely hate snakes. I used to spend the summer at my grandmother's house in the Rhone Valley, and there were lots of vipers around. Or so I was warned every day. 'You may go outside, child, but watch out for the serpents. They will rise up and strike your face.' I never saw a single snake but I developed a real snake phobia and quite a few slithery creatures in my dreams over the years, too."

"That must have been passed on to me—like osmosis. I wonder how many more of these wonderful inherited jewels lie in the depths of my psyche."

"I don't know what you are talking about, Isabelle. I never tried to make you afraid of anything. You can't blame me for all that happens to you in your life."

"I am not blaming you, Mother. I'm just saying that there are lots of things we don't understand and which sometimes stem from our family background. That's all. Just like we inherit a disposition for a certain disease or a trait of character from someone we've grown up with. You probably felt your grandmother's phobia of snakes very strongly and became afraid, yourself. It is that simple."

"Okay, you've got a point there. My grandmother got it from—who knows."

"That's what I mean."

"It's interesting, too, because I was thinking about the strong influence that the past has on this little town and what seems to float around in the air. It's as if the past did not want to die and the ghosts of the Gold Rush days still live among these walls and walk the old streets."

Isabelle chuckled. "Now it's my turn to ask: what you are talking about? Are you converting to some kind of spiritualism?"

Marguerite waved that thought away from the table. "Of course not, but there are things that spook me, sometimes, even in this place—maybe especially in this place."

"What, Mother?"

Marguerite paused and looked over at the stained glass window that was casting a soft red light into the room. "You know the furry scarf on the ground, next to the snake in your dream?"

"Yes?"

"That is probably the infamous ermine stole your grandmother, Mamie, kept in a trunk in her attic. It belonged to her sister, your grand aunt, who died in her fifties. There is some sort of a story about the stole but I forgot the details." She ate her croissant and thought. "Something about the two sisters' rivalry. But how in the world did this ermine stole get into your dream? What color was it?"

"A yellowish white, I think. Please, tell me more. I think it's important that I find out. Maybe this could explain some things about my state of mind these days."

"This stuff happened in the old country a long time ago and we're in America now, at the end of the twentieth century. There is no way this could relate to you."

"Mother, I want to find out some day."

Marguerite stood and began to clear the table. She paused then said. "I have an idea."

Isabelle gazed at her silently, waiting to hear more.

"We can talk about it later. I'm glad you slept well. I always think someone is walking around at night and it can get quite scary."

"Old wood has a tendency to creak. I guess I'd get scared too, if I lived here alone. How do you manage that?"

"It was strange at first but I've gotten used to it. Now I almost enjoy the company of my old friends parked within these brick walls. There are great legends hovering around here, you know, probably true stories."

"How come we never talked about all this before? I have been coming here for ages and you never said anything."

Isabelle's Dream

Her mother smiled softly. "Maybe you didn't hear me… you were always so involved with George, you did not talk much about anything else." She shrugged. "I kind of liked George. How is he?"

"I really don't know and I don't want to know. It's over for good, Mother, so please, don't bring him up again."

"Okay. Okay. How do you like my croissants? I prepared them yesterday, just needed to bake them at the last minute."

"They were great." Isabelle looked down at the table, back in yesterday's sullen mood, the same uncertainty washing away the simple pleasure of coffee, croissants, and strawberries. She looked up to find Marguerite watching her closely.

"Come with me to the basement, Isabelle. I want to show you something. I'll do the dishes later."

"So, what's so special about the basement?"

"You'll see—an old story about this town."

Intrigued, Isabelle followed her mother to a storage room adjacent to the store. There were more antiques there, scattered or piled up, most of them in need of restoration, all of them veiled with a thick dust. Marguerite pushed aside a small cabinet that concealed a trap door in the wood floor. She lifted it and descended carefully down a crude staircase. She promptly lit the room by pulling the string to a single bulb hanging from the basement's low beam ceiling.

"Be careful. There are a lot of nails on these steps. Stay on the right side where there's more light."

Isabelle joined her mother on the dirt floor of the cave-like space. It extended all the way under the store. There was nothing in it except for a couple of beat up trunks and some rusty tools.

"Why on earth did you bring me all the way down to this dirty place, Mother?"

"Do you see this plugged up tunnel?"

"What tunnel?"

"There on the street side, with some debris in front."

"Maybe. What is it?"

"They say that during the Gold Rush days this was a tunnel that led to the hotel across the street. Prostitutes used to come down from the saloon through the tunnel and go up to the storeroom that operated as a brothel. They also used to gamble in this basement. I bet you didn't know your mother lived in such an historic place! No wonder I hear voices sometimes."

Isabelle raised her eyebrows.

"Really, Isabelle, I do."

"You've got a terrific imagination, Mother."

"I knew I shouldn't tell you such things. You're such a skeptic. But remember, you hear voices, too, in your dreams."

"Okay, maybe there is something to it, especially if you believe it—believing it, that's the clue."

"I hear something now."

Isabelle listened and actually heard a distant knocking. It momentarily spooked her until she realized it was someone knocking on the front door of the shop. She looked at Marguerite's impish grin. "You are a complete rascal, Mother."

When the two women came back up from the basement, holding their robes up and somewhat disheveled from the dust and cobwebs, they found Naomi knocking desperately at the front door of the store.

"Where have you two been? I have been knocking for five minutes. I thought you both overslept. It's nine o'clock, do you realize?"

"Mother was showing me her ghosts' playground. I never thought a French woman would become that interested in the Gold Rush. Perhaps the prostitutes intrigued her."

"Oh, yes, the old tunnel and all that. It really happened, you know. Marguerite, you should show Isabelle China Gulch and tell her about the church."

"I will, and I don't care what you think, Isabelle. I truly am fascinated by history—any country's history."

"All right, let's go to the church. From the sinners to the sacred."

"Naomi, there's a man coming for the little porcelain doll, I hope."

"I'll be here. You go have fun."

China Gulch was not much of a place. The old buildings, occupied by the Chinese hands and cooks, had disappeared a long time ago, burned down with the town which had to be rebuilt several times. Gone also were the opium dens, which Marguerite informed, had done a steady business with the gold miners. The whole area behind the Hotel Leger had become, however, a privileged sort of a "banana belt" as a result of an unusually warm microclimate. There were fig and palm trees, as well as grapefruit and orange gardens. Isabelle closed her eyes and took in the fragrance. "Were these gardens here during the Gold Rush?" she asked. Marguerite nodded. "No wonder those scoundrels could thrive in this little oasis."

"I'm not sure they were all scoundrels. The Protestant church," her mother told her as they approached a narrow white building with a steeple and long thin windows, "was built with the proceeds from gold nuggets and gambling money collected by the town's charitable ladies."

"Do you suppose it was a memorial to lift the soul or appease the guilt?"

"Both, no doubt. It had burned down with the rest of the town in 1874, to be rebuilt later on. What do you think of all these places?"

"Not much left... but the legends are great."

"If you listen carefully... "

Marguerite took Isabelle through the two cemeteries where they read dates and facts on the tombstones, passed by the municipal park where every year people came from all over to attend the 4th of July celebrations complete with tug of war contests and parade. They walked by the old theater and the Hotel Leger, freshly repainted in pale yellow and white, its leaning balcony shading the street. "There is definitely something in the air getting under my skin," Isabelle admitted. "I can see why you like this place. It's enchanting in its simplicity. I'd never looked at it closely before."

"You've been a bit too rushed or distracted to notice until now."

"And I need to change that."

"I sold the doll," Naomi announced triumphantly when they returned to the store early afternoon, famished and tired.

"I showed Isabelle everything. Now she knows why we adore this place."

"By the way, how is George?" Naomi asked, innocently.

Marguerite signaled Naomi with her index finger on her lips while Isabelle, dispirited, ignored the question and walked quietly toward the apartment.

After dressing, Marguerite scurried between customers asking for help and her Provençal fish soup simmering on the kitchen stove. Isabelle settled in the little apartment and read a chapter in her psychology textbook for her evening class at U.C. extension. The windows were wide open, the spring air exhilarating. Sitting in her mother's living room with her feet up and totally immersed in the Mediterranean fragrances, Isabelle felt protected and warm. She felt childlike, with no other concerns but to come home after having played hard all day, knowing dinner would be delicious and her bed would be snug. She abandoned herself to the feeling. This was home as she once knew it, and it was good.

"I closed early, again, so we can have a long evening together," Marguerite announced cheerfully as she walked into the living room, interrupting Isabelle's reverie. "Business picked up a little. It usually does after Easter. The weekend tourists from the Bay area like to wander the hills this time of the year."

Dinner was tasty, the conversation much enhanced by a bottle of white Burgundy soothing enough to bring down anybody's defenses. The apartment was mellow and warm, and Isabelle let herself be pampered by her mother's loving care.

"What was that great idea you had this morning, Mother? We were talking about my dream, remember?"

"Ah, yes. You don't have to answer right away, of course." Marguerite paused and gazed at her daughter. "How would you feel about going to France this summer? I'm supposed to go and visit my mother in the late fall. She's not getting any younger, you know. She'll be ninety-four in September. I thought that, perhaps, you might want to go this summer, too? You could ask her all your questions about the old family stories. She is in a wheel chair most of the time, but she still lives at home with a woman guardian, someone like a nurse. Mamie has all of her marbles intact—she is really quite remarkable for her age and sometimes very funny."

Isabelle didn't answer right away. She sipped her wine. She hadn't seen her grandmother for at least three years when she had gone on a trip to Italy with George. At that time, her grandfather was still alive and they had lived in the family summer home in the small village of La Bâtie Montgascon. Isabelle's mind became flooded with visions of the rolling French countryside, a gracious old provincial home in the middle of a full blown park, a shady rugged path, a sleepy river, and the little cemetery she once visited where most of her maternal relatives rested.

She smiled in wonder at her sudden sense of excitement. "Actually, I would love it. I don't have any plans for the summer. George and I were going to go to Colorado for three weeks in July, but that's out, of course." She nodded with determination. "Okay, Mother. The trip sounds just perfect."

"Excellent. I'll come after you have to return for teaching, so she'll have lots of company this summer." Marguerite grinned and they clicked their wine glasses. "While you're over there, you have to visit the old Victor. He must be quite old by now. He once was the only doctor in the village, and he certainly had his own unorthodox ways to treat his patients."

"I don't remember him."

"He is a real character, I assure you. He knows a lot about the family. You might find him very informative, too. You can ask him anything. He always has answers—crazy ones, sometimes, but at least answers. You are going to have to brush up on your conversational French, Isabelle. You haven't spoken French for a long time."

Isabelle had learned French as her mother tongue when she was a little girl. Marguerite had tried to keep the language alive at home for a long time, but when she came to America, Isabelle started to resent being "different." The kids would make fun of her at school and she developed a strong dislike for speaking French, so she stopped all together. She was ashamed of her mother's accent, and only when she reached high school did she regain a certain respect for her French origins, especially when she became the best student in her language classes. Her pronunciation was perfect, better than her American teacher, and her direct contact with the culture—particularly the French pastries Marguerite would send with her for her friends to taste in class—made her a heroine. She spoke the language fairly well, but needed a lot more exposure to current idiomatic expressions.

"Well, I'll read *L'Express* for the next couple months."

"My immersion in the history around me has made me more aware of how I've neglected our own. I want to turn that around for both of us. This is so important to me, Isabelle, I'll pay for your trip."

Isabelle was stunned. "That is so generous, Mother. I don't know what to say."

"How about yes?"

Isabelle leaned over and kissed Marguerite on both cheeks. "Yes!"

SUNDAY MORNING, Isabelle decided to leave shortly after another lavish breakfast. She was ready to return to her own place and think about all that had happened in the few short days in the hills, from the dream to the winery that had inspired her mother to reminisce about the glorious daffodils and the ghostly town. Now, she would be taking a momentous journey back to her origins to face the strange images that perplexed her but, she knew, held answers for her future. She suddenly needed to digest it all in the quiet of her own home. Marguerite was disappointed that she had to leave earlier than usual, but Isabelle really did have a paper to prepare for her psychology class, and it made an honest excuse.

Isabelle packed her bag, kissed her mother on the right cheek and proceeded to walk toward her car.

"But Isabelle," Marguerite called after her, "you forgot the little wooden horse. I'll help you load it into the trunk."

"Thank you so much. I love it," Isabelle declared, huffing a little as they slung the beauty into her trunk.

Isabelle settled in for the drive home. She was upset and she knew it. She was glad she hadn't shown these feelings to her mother who had just offered her a wonderful trip to Europe. By the time she reached Highway 49, the disquieting questions started to besiege her. Her mother seemed so happy, so well adjusted in her surroundings. How did she do it? How could she settle for a life in such an insignificant place, away from city excitement? Was she truly happy or just pretending? What made her tick? She probably wouldn't ever get married again. Like Isabelle, she was probably looking ahead to long years of solitude. And why did Marguerite flaunt her "joie de vivre" in her daughter's face, when she very well knew that Isabelle had recently experienced a lot of pain. Isabelle felt suffocated by Marguerite's generous energy, and then she felt ridiculous and petulant, jealous of her mother's simple happiness.

Isabelle rolled the window down, realizing that she had been driving straight from Mokelumne Hill to Jackson in a state of concentrated painful uncertainty. Her shoulders were aching and her jaw was very tight. She took a deep breath, looking at the glorious landscape unfolding in front of her and immediately began to get some perspective without lashing out at Marguerite.

Why do I keep doing this to myself? she thought. Why can't I just live in the moment and enjoy my mother, even in her most overpowering solicitude. I could have stayed till the afternoon and instead, I am punishing myself, going home to be alone for the rest of the day. Why do I keep doing this to myself?

11

The Stream

Professor Handley smiled gently, almost teasingly. "I ask for an analysis of the difference between Jung and Freud with respect to childhood and I get your cinematic dream. I admit it kept my attention alive because it was witty and imaginative. But it's a little too romantic—the woman going to France in search of her past, hoping to discover her true self in a trunk in the attic, talking to a worn out grandmother and a sly family doctor. It probably won't change your life the way you hope it will. There is no such thing as magic. Also, although your paper is creative, it isn't exactly a psychological analysis."

Isabelle had anticipated his dismissal. "I think it is, by example. I think it's a dream about individuation. Freud believed we are slaves to our childhood trauma; Jung knew we are ever evolving. Of course, I understand that you cannot overturn deep-seated behaviors with a few revelations, but my dream was powerful enough to motivate me to begin this search. It unlocked something. It was frightening and intriguing at the same time. Could you help me figure out some of the images, Jungian style?"

"I would be happy to, Isabelle, but you know that dreams are strictly personal." Her psychology instructor did not fit the stereotype of a disengaged, paternal therapist. He looked more like a football coach because he was forty, very fit, with just a touch of gray at his temples. He always wore jeans, sneakers, and a crew neck sweater. Passing him on the street Isabelle would have dismissed him as shallow, but now she knew better. His brown eyes were penetrating and kind. He had deep knowledge in the field of psychology and great curiosity about the workings of the mind. "Dream interpretation," he continued, "rests ultimately on the dreamer, and except for some general archetypes, you'll have to decipher the meaning yourself."

"I understand." Isabelle opened her notebook to her account of the dream. "Let's start with the mirror."

"A reflection of the psyche trying to look into the unconscious to bring something to light."

"And the snake?"

"It could be a symbol for the unconscious again, or sometimes it means transformation. The snake holds strong energy, too. Your mother stirs up danger by kicking the snake, which bars the way to transformation. The danger would have to be resolved before the psyche can move on."

"Mother is negative?"

"Not exactly—it's a dream, remember, and the images are symbolic not literal. She is between you and knowledge represented by your ancestors."

"In real life, my mother is putting me in touch with my ancestors."

"She kicked the snake, opening an opportunity for entrance to the unknown."

"One last question: What does the scarf mean?"

Handley paused and leaned back in his desk chair with his hands behind his head. "I don't like to underestimate dreams. They can be prescient, meaning predict the future, or reveal information unavailable to the conscious mind. Perhaps your family's past worked its way into your unconscious and emerged in your dream through this image. You might find a clue to your individuation somewhere in the family history. There might even be an old ermine scarf in your grandmother's trunk." Handley smiled.

Isabelle grinned back at him. "Sounds like a little magic to me."

ISABELLE LEFT HANDLEY'S OFFICE feeling confident so she called George and left a message that he could meet her for lunch at the spa café after her workout. If it was inconvenient for him, too bad. She wanted to work out first, then to soak in the hot tub for a while. She knew that she could do some of her best thinking in the hot tub.

No one was in the women's area when she got to the Jacuzzi. She decided she would not turn on the jets, so that silence would help her relax more. She moved slowly down into the warm water, relishing the comforting feeling spreading all over her skin. She pictured herself in George's presence, big tall George with his large smile and his strong arms around her. She visualized him saying the magic words that had made her melt: "I missed you so much, baby. I love you. You know that I can't live without you." She reveled in the image of being precious to him, being loved. Then she suddenly saw the angry, drunken face of George, screaming at her, falling in bed, not being able to control himself. She felt her despair and hopelessness in front of this other picture. No, she was not the one responsible for this man's drinking problem. Isabelle would not let him back into her life, no matter how much he begged her— no matter how much she needed him. Isabelle was ready.

Isabelle's Dream

THE SPA HAD A SMALL CAFÉ, next to the pool. Most patrons were watching a basketball game on a large TV screen in the back of the room, and they did not even look at Isabelle when she walked in, dressed in a cheerful yellow sweat suit. She spotted George sitting at a table by the window on the street side. He looked as if he had gained a little weight. He was wearing a stylish brown leather jacket over a beige shirt, and his grey hair was carefully brushed and his beard trimmed shorter than she remembered it. He looked handsome. George smiled when he saw her. Isabelle noticed immediately a single red rose on the place mat in front of her seat. "Oh, I'm in trouble," she thought. "I hope I can handle this," and she walked toward him.

"Isabelle, you look stunning. What did you do to yourself?"

"Just worked out and took a Jacuzzi. Hello, George, it's good to see you."

George hugged Isabelle warmly, and for a moment, she remembered her grandfather who gave her the same kind of a big bear hug. It was hard to resist, so she didn't, letting herself enjoy the comfortable embrace. George was wearing Old Spice aftershave, a lot of it. She pushed him gently back and sat down.

"What will you have to eat, Isabelle?"

"Let me see. A cup of the daily soup, whatever it is. I'll drink water."

George called the waitress and gave Isabelle's order. He wanted a hamburger for himself with French fries and a small salad. "I'll drink water, too" he said jokingly. "See what love can do to a man?"

Isabelle did not answer, and she did not know what to do with the rose. She finally lifted it, smelled it while looking at George with a thankful expression, nodded, and then put it on the corner of the table.

George looked nervous. He began to fidget. Isabelle's silence did not make the situation any easier for him. He kept looking at her, trying to summon the best words he could find, and then he plunged in.

"You don't know how much I missed you, baby. These last months have been the hardest in my life. I am lost without you. I love you so much. I think of you all the time. Could we try again? Isabelle, my sweet, I want so much to give our relationship another chance. Could we try again? What do you say?"

Isabelle listened to the expected words, without melting this time, watching this man she had needed so much tell her that he needed her now, and she felt sorry for him.

"You know how I feel about it, George, and it hasn't changed. I just couldn't go on the way it was between us, with your changes of mood, your drinking, and all that."

"But you don't know how much I have changed. I've cut down on my drinking. I feel that I can handle it. You'll see. Just give me another chance."

Isabelle felt sad for this big strong man sitting in front of her, begging. "I gave you many chances, George," she said softly. "If I were to get back with you, I would have to be sure that you quit your drinking for good, that you'd promise to go to therapy. Would you?"

"But I cut down, Isabelle. You can't ask me to quit cold turkey, just like that. I'll need some time. You'll be my best therapy. Come back," he dropped his voice, "and I'll make the sweetest love to you."

Isabelle knew that he could. He was a very good lover and she missed sex in her life very much. She was tempted to just say, "Let's go home and make love right now." Her heart was beating fast and her face was flushed. She wanted George to take her in his arms and carry her away—but then she remembered the promise she had made to herself in the hot tub. If she gave in right now, and the relationship returned to what it was before, as it probably would, how would she feel?

"You're not saying anything, Isabelle. What are you thinking about?"

"George, I'm sorry, but I don't want to get back together. I can't live with an alcoholic anymore."

Isabelle couldn't believe she had uttered the word alcoholic, quietly, gently, but eloquently. It was the first time she had been able to do it, and it had not been that difficult. She took a deep breath.

George threw up his arms. "I am not an alcoholic," he shouted, "and I can't take your accusations anymore."

He stood and she noticed that his jacket pocket bulged a little. It was the shape of a pint bottle. She pointed at it.

He paused and quickly covered his pocket with his hand. For a second he looked embarrassed. Then he scowled again and hissed, "The hell with you, Miss Perfect." He scurried out of the coffee shop just as the waitress was bringing their order.

"What happened to the gentleman?" she asked.

"He didn't feel well; he had to go. I'll eat my lunch here and I will take his in a take-out bag, okay?"

Isabelle tried to sip her soup, but it caught in her throat. As ridiculous as it was that he came to reconcile with a bottle of booze in his pocket,

George had pushed the right button. Was she really "Miss Perfect," trying to make him fit into a mold? Perfectionism—the very thing she had accused her mother of. No, she did not have to take the blame. It was simple: She did not want to live with an alcoholic.

Isabelle felt better and started eating her lunch. "I'll do something nice for myself this afternoon," she congratulated herself, "I deserve it." As she finished her meal, she thought about the trip to Europe. By rejecting George, she had opened a big door to her future. As what? A better French teacher? A more equal partner in a future relationship? A better friend to her mother? Simply a member of a family she had lost a long time ago but still resided in her psyche?

The waitress brought the take-out with her check.

With a wave of her hand, Isabelle said, "On second thought, I don't want his food. Just give it to someone else or throw it away." The waitress shrugged and left it on the table.

"I am going to give myself a party this evening. I just got rid of a worst part of my past: my dependence on a man," Isabelle said under her breath, and on her way home she stopped at Petrini's, bought a salmon filet, some asparagus, a baguette, a bottle of Beaujolais, and some candles. At the bakery, she purchased a large slice of a beautiful chocolate and raspberry cake.

When she got home, Isabelle found a note pinned on her door. It said, "If you don't have anything better to do, stop by my place for dinner this evening. Call me before 3 pm if you can." It was signed Catharine. Catharine was Isabelle's best friend and the two women often got together on very short notice. Isabelle checked her watch; it was two thirty. She picked up the phone and dialed Catharine's number. "Guess what? I've got a great dinner for tonight, wine and all. You come to my place instead and we'll celebrate."

"What are we celebrating?"

"You'll see. Six o'clock."

Isabelle started preparing her classes for the next few days. The end of the semester was approaching and it was difficult to keep the students' attention, she had to be more imaginative than ever to do it. "I'll have one class with French readings and vocabulary about snakes," she thought. "It always fascinates the kids and I might learn something in the process, too. I'll have them write about their summer plans, too, and what they can do to respect nature and the environment." Since it was pleasantly warm, Isabelle also decided to teach some of her classes outside on the lawn by the playground. Her students would love her for it.

When Catharine walked in, late as usual, the room brightened. She was short and a little plump, with striking blond hair and blue eyes, a wonderful smile and a deep tan that she cultivated year-round. Catharine was a lively Dutch woman just a little older than Isabelle. She had come to the U.S. in the fifties as a student from Holland, had married here and raised two sons who were now in their late twenties. Her husband Simon had died in a car accident ten years ago. The two women met at a teacher's workshop and became very good friends. The pragmatic Catharine was a good complement for romantic Isabelle, and they shared their innermost feelings freely. They went to movies and concerts, spent some time doing volunteer work together. They had even traveled to Mexico together once when Isabelle was between men.

"Hello, Dahling," said Catharine as she hugged Isabelle with a motherly effusion. "So good of you to invite me. Look what we have here. This is the cutest little horse I have ever seen."

"I just brought it back from the antique shop. I fell in love with it, so Marguerite gave it to me."

"You are so lucky to have your mother here in America, I wished mine were a little closer. Look what you've done!" Catharine pointed to the dining room table set with a pink tablecloth and matching napkins, light green earthenware dishes, green goblets, silverware, and two green candles. "Are we going to savor your traditional tuna fish sandwich in style today?"

"All right Catharine, you continue like this and I won't tell you what we are celebrating."

"Come on, I was just joking. I know you can cook when you want to. So, what are we having?"

"A party Catharine, a real party. I was going to give it to myself alone, but since you are joining me, we'll both celebrate."

Isabelle poured two glasses of wine and lifted hers to make a toast.

"To two wonderful women and their upcoming adventures."

Catharine looked at her sideways. "Isabelle, what's happened? What adventures?"

Isabelle proceeded to tell Catharine at great length the topic of her conversation with George and what had resulted from it.

"I am proud of you. I always told you that George was a boozer in denial but you wouldn't listen to me. You kept trying to reform him. You finally got the message."

"But he looked so pitiful." Isabelle covered her mouth so she wouldn't laugh. "You should have seen his sad eyes. He was almost crying—until I said the A word, at which point anger kicked in with a vengeance. And listen to this. I saw a pint in his pocket. Can you believe he couldn't even come to reconcile without it?"

"Just forget about the guy. I don't think he'll ever dry out. Now that you've made the final, definite, terminal break, you take care of yourself, Isabelle. You hear me?"

"I hear you, Catharine. I hear you loud and clear." Isabelle took another sip of her wine while Catharine rummaged through her purse looking for cigarettes. She would go outside on the patio to smoke it because Isabelle was not a smoker and she did not like fumes around her house. Catharine stepped out to indulge in her craving while Isabelle started to bring dinner on the table and light the candles.

"So, we are celebrating your new found power," said Catharine impishly, as she walked back in and sat down at the table. "I was wondering how long it would take you to really learn how to say no. Why is it so hard for you to do that?"

Isabelle did not answer her question but started to unfold her napkin with a mysterious look on her face. "Now, for the rest of the celebration. Catharine, I had the greatest idea. I am going to France this summer to visit my grandmother and retrace the family past, as you know. So I thought, why don't you go to Holland to visit your mother at the same time? We could travel together, fly to Paris for instance, spend a few days there, and then we would meet at the end of the trip and come back together."

"So that's the adventure you were talking about. This could be fun indeed." Catharine laughed. "Maybe we could both have an affair while we're there. I'll drink to that!"

"Catharine! I've never heard you talk like that."

"And why not? Life is short; we have to make the best of it! You agree?"

"Of course, but you don't make an affair happen just like that. You meet, fall in love, and maybe wonderful things happen."

"You are a hopeless romantic, Isabelle."

"That's what my psychology teacher said to me. I was embarrassed."

"He sure was right. We all know that."

The two women ate their dinner with great gusto. Catharine complimenting Isabelle on her choice of fresh wild salmon, which she had baked with ginger, green onions, and white wine.

"You see Isabelle, you can cook. It was delicious."

"Well, I am not a Marguerite in the kitchen, but I like to experiment."

PLANNING FOR THE TRIP OVER DESSERT kept them laughing with the promise of a fine adventure. They decided on a departure date and on the length of time they would spend in Paris: one week sounded about right, and then they would go their separate ways and meet again at Charles De Gaulle airport three weeks later for the flight back.

"Do you realize how lucky we are, Catharine, to be financially self-sufficient women? I was thinking of all these women who stay in a relationship just because they can't make it on their own. They may have to face an alcoholic husband or a physically abusive partner and stay with them nevertheless. They may spend their whole lives this way, not daring to get out."

"And then there are some who are financially independent but who stay, just the same, because they don't dare to say no."

Isabelle shrugged with a wave of her hand. "Yes. I can relate to them. They can't be without a man. They need a man to make them whole. I'm learning the hard way the trick is to become whole first, and then you have a better chance of falling into the right relationship."

Catharine gazed into her glass of wine. "Simon was a wonderful husband. I suppose we were both very independent. We actually didn't spend that much time together, but when we did, things were sweet." She paused. "It's been ten years, now. I still miss him a lot."

"I am sorry Catharine. I didn't mean to bring the conversation to a sad place for you. Forgive me."

"Forgive you, for what? You made an excellent dinner, the wine was superb, we are planning a trip to Europe this summer, and your friendship is precious to me. Life is good, Isabelle."

Isabelle looked at her friend carefully then reached over and squeezed her hand. "Yes Catharine, life is good."

After Catharine left, she listened to Bach's Air on a G String while she did the dishes. The kitchen window was open and a fresh cool breeze caressed her face. She looked out; a small crescent moon was rising behind the elm grove. "What a beautiful night!" she whispered. She caught herself washing the green plates to the rhythm of the music. Not being able to resist any longer, she abandoned the sink and danced her way into the living room,

Isabelle's Dream

putting her joy in every smooth step. Jasmine watched her from a perch on the back of the antique horse. "I don't care what they all say," Isabelle told her pet. "I love being a romantic."

III

The Women

When the two women arrived in Paris about 10 a.m., tired, jetlagged, and disoriented, they were greeted by an unromantically overcast sky. Caught up in the commotion of Charles de Gaulle Airport and the noise of passengers being greeted by relatives, they proceeded in a daze toward the exit. Everything around them looked dim and grey.

"That's our luck," Catharine declared grumpily as they stepped outside into a drizzle. "I sure hope it won't rain the whole time we're in Paris."

Isabelle shivered and pulled a sweater and umbrella from her handbag. "We're Californians. We forget that there is such a thing as rain."

They stood in line for a taxi but a loud couple from New York pushed them aside as a shiny Mercedes pulled to the curb. The next cab was a dented Peugeot. The exuberant driver jumped out and grabbed their bags saying, "I take! I take! Welcome," as he tossed their luggage into the trunk.

When they were seated in the back, he looked back over the seat with a leering grin. "I am Yasir. Where to go?"

"Hotel Scandinavia, 17 Rue de Tournon in the Latin Quarter." Isabelle whispered to Catharine, "Marguerite discovered this place years ago. It's 300 years old."

Catharine looked at her ruefully. "I hope it's in better shape than this Peugeot."

Yasir checked a very torn, wrinkled city map with a scowl, and then he jabbed at it and tossed it onto the seat. He threw the Peugeot into gear and squealed away from the curb, barely missing a minivan from the Paris Hilton. Isabelle grabbed the door handle with one hand and Catharine's arm with the other.

Yasir talked nonstop, his unkempt curly black hair flying right and left, his hands flying on and off the steering wheel as he threw curses at passing cars in a language Isabelle didn't understand. He kept his window down and the noise of speeding cars and motorcycles was deafening. Yasir cut in and out of lines so close to other cars that Isabelle shivered in her seat. Catharine simply looked straight ahead with a fixed stare.

The Parisian landscape unfolded very slowly. Nondescript buildings, billboards, flashing signs told tourists how many minutes they were away from Porte Maillot or the Arc de Triomphe. In standstill traffic, an ambulance screamed behind them. It passed so close to the taxi that Yasir tapped its side as it squeezed between the lanes.

"Ah, you see lady. Look, futbol!" She pointed to a large soccer stadium on their left, Yasir looked back them. "World Cup, you know?" Isabelle nodded curtly. The taxi was rolling too quickly toward a car stopped in front of them. Isabelle gasped. Yasir looked forward and slammed on the brakes. He cursed and then laughed heartily, letting a stream of Moroccan or Pakistani or Egyptian words flow from him like marbles onto the street.

The hill of Montmartre Sacré Coeur appeared in the distance. Catharine sighed and Isabelle realized her friend had been terrified, too, in spite of her nonchalant attitude.

Yasir looked back at them again. "Misses alone in big city? Yasir show you all, no? I come to hotel and show you?"

"No thank you. We like to walk."

"Oh, not good for woman alone." He scowled back at them.

"We'll be fine."

"Not good woman alone." Yasir shook his hand across the seat. "Yasir come hotel and show you all."

Catharine and Isabelle glanced at each other, each feeling the menace behind his tone but bristling at the age-old suggestion that women shouldn't travel alone.

"We like to walk," repeated Catharine. Fortunately, they passed the Palais du Luxembourg before he could answer and a block later pulled up in front of the hotel. Located between the Boulevard Saint-Germain and the Luxembourg Gardens, the Scandinavian had a Middle Ages motif. Two statues of knights in full body armor guarded each side of the main door. Against her spirit of independence, Isabelle felt reassured by their antique protective demeanor.

Catharine checked the meter and pulled out some francs. Yasir tossed their suitcases on the sidewalk with a thump, mumbling about women and tourists. Before he jumped back in the cab he hollered, "Yasir show you Paris. I come." Then he squealed away from the curb barely missing a delivery truck.

They each picked up a suitcase and headed for the lobby past the formidable medieval guards. "*Bonjour*," Isabelle nodded at the one on her right. Catharine looked at her like she was nuts. The concierge was a young blond dressed in a peasant costume, but she had a tattoo of a snake on her very visible breast. A Coke machine stood behind the counter. She checked their passports and gave them a key, pointing to the stairs. "Third floor, on the left."

The women climbed the 300-year-old steps to their room. In spite of the ultra-modern concierge, their bedroom was very Parisian, rather small, clean, and cheerful, with an open beam ceiling and some Cocteau prints on the walls. The bathroom was tiny by American standards and Isabelle and Catharine bumped into each other as they picked respective sides of the room, hung up their clothes in the huge armoire, and settled into their home for the week in Paris.

Catharine pulled aside the curtain. A tall, thin, multi-paned window looked out on a row of beautiful seventeenth-century stone buildings. "Quaint, isn't it?" she said.

"It's the ideal spot for our Parisian week." Isabelle sat on her bed and sighed a weary traveler's sigh. "It's funny, though, when I had imagined our trip, I visualized this beautiful postcard image of the city, with monuments outlined against a gorgeous blue sky, a plush hotel with antique furniture, satin curtains, and soft carpeting, a mysterious concierge at the desk, looking up from behind his half-rimmed glasses to inspect *les américains*. Yet here we are, in glorious Paris, where everything is sad and grey, the room is small, and... "

Catharine gave her a quick pat on the shoulder. "Oh, you're just a little tired and hungry, Isabelle. It's to be expected."

"That annoying cabbie didn't set a mood of *joie de vivre*, did he?"

"You'll feel much better about Paris after you get some rest and have a lovely meal."

"You're absolutely right." Isabelle got up and lifted her suitcase on a luggage stand. They each bathed, put on fresh, comfortable clothes, and then Catharine closed the curtains against the now sunlit Parisian morning. Stretching out on their cozy, narrow beds, they dropped off to sleep.

They slept soundly for several hours and it was mid-afternoon when they woke up, well rested. Catharine drew the heavy curtains back with renewed vigor. "Bright sunshine!"

"Paris, here we come," exclaimed Isabelle, jumping out of bed. "I'm starving."

The lobby was empty as they walked across the stylish black and white tiles. Isabelle saluted the armored doorman, and they headed down the Rue de Touron. They bought a baguette at a small bakery a block from the hotel. Next door, a small shop sold groceries. With cheese, fruit, and baguette in hand, they walked through Luxembourg Garden admiring statues of the queens of France, lush flower beds, and centuries-old trees.

"This is the Paris I imagined." Isabelle smiled from ear to ear.

"Let's sit on this bench and eat. I can't walk another step without some of that artisan cheese." As they broke off hunks of bread and cheese, they admired the Garden. Children were launching their boats in a basin, two lovers were kissing on a bench, and fountains were gurgling on every side of them. They were in a foreign land but by the simple act of two friends eating their snack on a wrought iron bench in a public park, they now felt a part of it.

From the Garden, they walked through the Latin quarter, down Saint-Michel Boulevard to the Musée National du Moyen Age, fascinated by everything they encountered: the way Parisians park their cars on sidewalks to the abundant merchandise displayed in the stores lining the avenue. In the museum, they went into the sunken Gallo-Roman ruins of the third-century Thermes Public Baths.

"Imagine when these baths were in use."

"Such layers of history around here. Remember when the students fought the May '68 revolution, tearing all the cobblestones from Saint-Michel Boulevard pavement to throw at cars and shop windows?"

"I was shocked. I never would have done anything like that," said Isabelle.

Catharine shrugged. "I demonstrated against the Vietnam War at Berkeley. That was pretty intense, too."

They sat by Saint-Michel Fountain for a while, next to people speaking many different languages, silently taking in the cosmopolitan unity. Both decided that Rue Saint Séverin around Saint Séverin Church was the most enjoyable, because it was completely reserved for pedestrian traffic in a very old part of the quarter. "Some of the houses have walls that date back to the 13th century," Isabelle read from a pamphlet. Scores of small ethnic restaurants lined the narrow cobblestone street, giving it a party atmosphere. Catharine and Isabelle decided to have dinner at an inviting bistro, where they sat outside, looking at the stunning old church. "There are only American tourists eating here," whispered Catharine to Isabelle as she sipped a glass of Chardonnay.

"No wonder. It's six o'clock! French people usually eat dinner much later."

"We'll get used to it. Now we just need to get over our jet lag. What shall we do first tomorrow?"

Isabelle's Dream

Isabelle thought while the waiter brought a bowl of onion soup for her and pan-seared halibut for Catharine. "I don't want to see the usual Parisian landmarks like the Eiffel Tower, Notre Dame, and the Louvre. We'd stand in line and bump elbows with the crowds for hours."

"Anyway, how many times have you seen the Vénus de Milo?"

Isabelle laughed. "Too many times. I'd like to be a little more adventuresome, follow our intuition and find a different Paris."

The evening was young, the air balmy. Comforted by their meal, the two women walked into Saint Séverin Church, marveling at the twisted pillar that holds the church's vault, the beautiful modern stained glass window behind the altar, and the quiet Middle Age cloister on the west side with its mossy arches and weathered statues. Isabelle lit a candle in the church. She liked the ritual of the little wavering flame, burning in the darkness, while she would think of someone in need of a prayer. She thought of George but dismissed blessing him because he was a bombastic jerk. Instead, she sent good wishes to a student of hers who had been in a car accident. The girl was paralyzed but full of wit and determination. Isabelle admired her and sent her good will from the spirit of Saint Séverin

Back on the streets, they tuned into the Rue du Chat qui Pêche (Street of the Fishing Cat) where they could barely walk side by side between the dark houses.

"I feel like I'm in a time warp."

"We've been transported back 500 years. Watch out, Isabelle! Someone might throw their slop pot from upstairs."

"Oh stop. You almost had me running to the next *rue.*"

Catharine spread her arms out. "It's so narrow I can touch each wall."

Though they weren't tired at all and their inside clock was telling them it was only midday in California, Isabelle and Catharine decided to head back to the hotel go to bed early. They knew the only cure for jet lag was to wake up at a natural hour the second day.

They slept well and woke up to a grey sky. "It'll clear up," said Catharine over breakfast at a nearby café. "It did yesterday."

"Paris has a climate of its own."

"Let's go to the Catacombs," Catharine suggested with great enthusiasm.

"It's so morbid, Catharine, you are sure that you want to see that on such a gloomy morning?"

"They're fascinating. In Rome, catacombs were underground places where the first Christians hid from persecution. Later, they were used to store bones. Here, the Catacombs were a huge underground stone quarry that later became a repository for bones taken out of cemeteries. There were so many people in Paris that they had to make room for more and more bodies. Paris is over two thousand years old, so that made for quite a pile of bones." Catharine laughed.

"I don't know. My mother took me to the basements of her ghost town. Now you're taking me to crypts beneath the city. Are you two pushing me to my grave? I'm not *that* old."

"Life and death where ever you go. It will be an adventure. Think, Isabelle, when will you be able to see something like this again? I love to go underground but I promise you this: I won't drag you to the Paris sewers… although they are very famous, you know."

"Yeah, yeah, the Phantom of the Opera and all that! Okay, we'll see the catacombs today, but tomorrow, I choose our destination."

As they left the café, Catharine paused and put her hand on Isabelle's arm. "Look across the street."

Isabelle followed her friend's gaze. Yasir leaned against his battered Peugeot watching them. He nodded grimly. "I show Paris." He opened the back door of the taxi and gestured for them to get in.

Isabelle turned to walk away but Catharine crossed the street in a few bold strides. "Listen. We told you yesterday we don't want to take a cab. What are you doing here?"

He looked away from her direct stare. "Women need guide."

"No, we don't."

"Yes."

"No."

Isabelle decided the argument was going to get out of hand. "Yasir," she said in a friendly tone, "American women travel alone all the time. Surely you know this."

He shook his dark curls and gestured into the back seat more forcefully as if his hands could express his opinion better than his broken English.

How strange that he's so persistent, she thought. He's either a nut case or it's about something in his life. "Does your wife live in Paris?"

Yasir looked at her with shock, frowned, and answered gruffly, "No, in Libya."

"That's too bad. Is she alone?"

"No. Good family. I send money."

"But you miss her."

"I send money." He suddenly dropped his shoulders and looked deeply sad.

"You are taking good care of her from a distance. You should go visit her."

Catharine interrupted. "Isabelle, this is all very interesting but let's move on."

Isabelle nodded. "Goodbye Yasir. Thank you but we don't want a taxi."

The man shrugged and shut the back door.

As they crossed the street back to the sidewalk, they heard him start the engine and drive away.

"I'm touched."

"I'm annoyed. I don't want to be followed in Paris. It's creepy."

"True. But it's a reality that so many men have to leave their families to earn money. I guess I've always thought of it as being an adventure for the men and a hardship for the women left behind."

"Well, it's both. But let's go enjoy ourselves in the pile of bones."

When they arrived at the entrance to the Catacombs indicated in their guidebook, it was some sort of a low metal door resembling a large manhole. They were the first ones in line. Isabelle fell into a strange quiet mood after the encounter with Yasir, but Catharine chatted cheerily with three German tourists from Dresden and a young couple from Belgium. A guide unlocked the door and gave each of them a candlestick. One by one, they descended a steep narrow stairway beside dark stone walls. At the bottom of the steps, they slowly walked down a long dank corridor, listening to the sound of water running through an invisible viaduct. They came to a portal with a plaque that read: "*Arrête, c'est ici l'empire de la mort*" (Stop, this is the empire of death). As they entered the ossuary, walls on each side held hundreds of niches and bins filled with bones of all sizes. Some were sorted out, like the skulls, others just thrown together. The guide told them several shafts that originated from the main corridor, going in other directions, were very likely filled with more niches and bins. There were warning signs against venturing into these shafts and getting lost. Isabelle shivered, and she held on tighter to her candle hoping a little of its warmth would flow into her. Now and then, a panel engraved with one of Pascal's quotes about death compounded the somber atmosphere of the place. The dim flickering candlelight projected against the sinister walls and added to the darkness and sense of the futility of life.

The group of tourists arrived at some sort of a crossroad where several passages meet, a round room with an altar in the middle. The guide said in a disinterested monotone, "Masses are said here sometimes, especially on the day of the Dead in November." He held his candle below his face and it made his eyes look deep and skeletal. He looked like an incarnation of the bones around them. Isabelle looked right and left for a way out but only saw more bones. She felt that she was taking a trip not just through the remains of six million Parisians but deep into an underworld from which she might never return. The corridors went on and on; the candles slowly burned down. In this macabre maze, it became clear to Isabelle why humans liked so much to light candles in church. It was the antithesis to the Catacombs: life, warmth, and light.

When they finally came out at the exit located one mile from the entrance, Isabelle sighed and stretched, realizing how her muscles had pulled tight during the journey through ten centuries of death. "I thought I'd never escape."

Catharine had a glint in her eyes. "Don't be silly. It was exotic and magical."

"Dark magic, though."

"I'm famished. Let's find another one of those cozy bistros."

The sky was still overcast but not raining. Isabelle at first couldn't fathom the idea of eating, especially not meat, but when they sat down she discovered she was famished after the long walk and gobbled up two pieces of bread dipped in olive oil. She ordered a Niçoise salad and Catharine devoured an omelet.

"What next?" asked Catharine, sipping an espresso in a tiny white cup.

"Fresh air," said Isabelle with a laugh, "even if it pours rain."

After lunch, they hopped the Métro down to the Seine to walk along the river. The Pont Neuf is the oldest bridge in Paris, built in the 16th century. They almost had to bend over to walk under its vault. They sat in the little garden Vert-Galant with a beautiful view of the Seine where it splits into two arms embracing the Ile de la Cité.

"The island is where Paris began."

"Wasn't the ossuary fascinating this morning?" asked Catharine, still under the spell of the catacombs.

"Interesting is more like it. I prefer gardens like this."

"But, think, Isabelle. Paris is not only the city above ground; it is also this incredible infrastructure of Métro lines crisscrossing the town on three superimposed levels sometimes, and then there's the network of sewer systems, the catacombs, the remains of the original city, several times built over. I tell you, I am fascinated by this giant underground web, invisible to us sitting on top of it while it trembles with life under our very feet."

"Life perhaps but so much death, too. I guess it is important to sense that, but it is my turn to choose the attraction tomorrow, Catharine. Let's go to Giverny."

ISABELLE HAD ALWAYS WANTED to go to Giverny, home of Impressionist Claude Monet. The bus ride was pleasant, partly following the river and crossing through small towns. Isabelle liked Monet's painting very much. She had seen several of his works in San Francisco at the touring exhibit and also at the Musée de l'Orangerie during a previous trip to Paris. She was fascinated by the ghost-like quality of his London "Houses of Parliament," his Venice in "The Doges Palace seen from San Giorgio" and Rouen's many Cathedral paintings, where he played with the light so well that the buildings become immaterial, blending with their surroundings, in an almost ephemeral way. Now Isabelle wanted to see where Monet had spent the latter part of his life, after he partially lost his eyesight, and where he painted the famous water lilies and the Japanese footbridge.

Monet, the founder of Impressionism, had once said, "My finest masterpiece is my garden." Planted with exotic flowers, weeping willows, bamboo trees and rhododendrons, the garden also offered the visitor all the flowers in season, meticulously kept by inconspicuous gardeners who blended them skillfully together, in sizes and colors, to make the premises appear to be a huge painting. All the blues and the pinks and the reds and the yellows of flowers, whose names Isabelle didn't even know, were blossoming, mixed wildly together in well-planned large beds. The roses were in full bloom, and the two women wandered in awe through alleys of the most stunning specimens. Crossing under the street, through the tunnel, they arrived on the other side, at the famous pond, spanned by the blue-green Japanese footbridge. The water lilies were floating on the pond as they did seventy years ago, with the weeping willows casting their undulating shadows on the water. It was the most beautiful and peaceful sight.

Isabelle and Catharine sat on a bench for a while, taking it all in. Isabelle closed her eyes and recalled the sense of renewal she experienced in the fields of Daffodil Hills. Monet would have appreciated the yellow-green palate offered in the California daffodils. A powerful moment in the world of art had emerged here at Giverny, based on the same abundance of the natural world. Monet's late paintings of this pond, seen through his sickly eyes, had produced the strangest, strongest blend of brush strokes and colors that revealed the substance of life flowing within the plants. Isabelle instinctively knew that what Monet wanted to—and did—capture on the canvas; it was identical to her own resonance with nature and part of her quest.

Catharine tapped her arm, awakening Isabelle from her reverie. She pointed at a tall, gray-haired gentleman standing near them. He was carrying a camera and gestured taking a photo. Catharine shrugged. "Why not?"

Isabelle and Catharine posed on the footbridge. The gentleman took three or four shots and said with a wink, "*Je prends une photo de deux belles femmes dans une belle endroit.*"

"What did he say?" asked Catharine.

"He's flirting. He says he took a photo of two beautiful women in a lovely place."

Catharine whispered, "He's kind of cute."

"Come on. Let's get some lunch before you do something you'll regret."

They waved goodbye. "*Merci, merci,*" he said and elegantly bowed.

Giggling at his extravagant antics, the women walked around the gardens another hour and then ate a late lunch at a small restaurant nearby. They ordered a simple but delicious combination of fresh baked bread, local cheeses, cold cuts, and pâté. They drank a local cider and marveled at how well they had eaten since they arrived in France.

"This is why the French are so healthy. Tons of fat but it's all local."

"And we walk everywhere." Catharine groaned and leaned down to massage her foot.

Isabelle paid the bill and they crossed the street to catch their bus back to the Latin Quarter. During the ride back to Paris, Isabelle and Catharine were quiet and pensive, a mood that stayed with them for the rest of the evening. It was difficult to talk after being surrounded in such compelling, gentle gardens, and words felt superfluous.

They woke up the following day to a bright blue sky. After a late breakfast of fresh croissants and café au lait in their room, the two women felt ready to conquer Paris. They started talking about a few of the places they wanted to see.

Catharine thumbed through her guidebook. "What about visiting the Père Lachaise Cemetery. Everybody famous is buried there: Balzac, Sarah Bernhardt, Maria Callas…

"She had a stunning voice."

Catharine smiled. "Ah, I've got you on the hook. Delacroix, Édith Piaf, Chopin… "

"That's not fair. You know I love Chopin and Piaf. But even so, after yesterday, I can't go back to the world of the dead. I tell you what, you go there and enjoy it, and I'll wander along the Seine, around the Bouquinistes area. We can meet later in the afternoon for an early dinner and go to the concert at Saint-Julien le Pauvre Church. What do you think?"

"It's a deal. I'll miss you and you'll probably regret that you did not come along."

"It's a bit new for me to claim what I want to do. I couldn't do this with the men in my life. Whatever they wanted… "

"That's men. Always with the guilt-tripping. We're friends Isabelle. Doing different things is not a problem. As a matter of fact, it'll be fun to compare notes later."

STILL A LITTLE STUNNED that it had been so easy to do what she wanted without creating a drama, Isabelle followed the right bank of the Seine. At her leisure she wandered from one book stall to the next, picking up prints and old cards, leafing through books, talking to the vendors, watching boats going down the river and fishermen trying their luck in the murky waters. She heard a cacophony of birds and followed the sound across the street to find a bird shop. Perches were lined with canaries, finches, parakeets, and parrots of all sorts. The small aviaries sounded like live jungles. With childlike wonder she watched them prune and peck and flutter. Playfulness lightened her step and she window-shopped aimlessly. Soon she saw the giant Samaritaine department store near the Pont Neuf. It was named for a 17th century water pump with a bas-relief of the Samaritan woman drawing water for Jesus at the well as described in the Gospel of St. John. Isabelle saw a chic hat on a mannequin in the display window and spontaneously entered the store. For an hour, she tried on outrageous outfits, hats and all, just for fun, making faces and funny poses, like models would do, in front of the full-length mirrors. Suddenly she realized Catharine was expecting her at the Chatelet Métro exit. Isabelle trotted as fast as she could and found her friend waiting for her on a bench outside the station. When Catharine picked her out from the crowd, she tapped her watch in mock annoyance.

"So, have you been playing so hard today that you almost forgot me?"

"I'm so, so sorry, Catharine. I didn't mean… "

"Oh stop, Isabelle. I'm kidding. I've actually loved sitting here watching the faces in the crowds. See that man over there feeding the pigeons. He's nutty as a fruitcake."

They started walking towards the Saint-Julien le Pauvre Church. "How was the visit to the city of death?"

"It was amazing. They are all there: Molière, La Fontaine, Appollinaire, and your favorites, Edith Piaf and Chopin. Writers, poets, musicians, painters. It is almost as gorgeous at Giverny, landscaped with trees and flowers. There are little chapels where people are buried inside, some very elaborate tombstones with photos on them. I met a Danish woman who was taking notes and pictures of the place. She told me some of the stories about the cemetery, like the one about this young man who was in love with the picture of a beautiful woman buried there, and he would visit the grave every day and bring flowers. One day, her spell was so strong that he committed suicide. There is also a stone statue of an exquisitely handsome young man. It is said that women who want children come and caress his penis. Now it's all worn away by their hopeful rubbing hands. This whole place has some strong vibes, I tell you. I had a marvelous time."

"Catharine, why you are so fascinated by places like these?"

Catharine paused. "I guess it is because of the war. I am older than you are, you know, and I was a child in Holland during the last war. We saw a lot of dead people. Death became part of our child's play, burying bugs, dead animals, even dolls. It was something we had to do. We'd decorate the graves and make them beautiful and do processions and singing like for funerals. We even buried my friend's brother, once, but we let his head stick out."

"How awful."

"He didn't mind; actually he was very flattered that we chose him. We certainly lavished him with attention. So that's probably why I've kept a certain fascination for death. I look for the spirit of people when I visit a gravesite. I can feel it."

"I am sorry, Catharine."

"There is nothing to be sorry about. I'm not sad. This is just part of life, Isabelle. Perhaps I think about it more often than other people do, but not in a morbid way."

The two women passed a seafood restaurant along the river where they ordered a *plateau de fruits de mer*, an elaborate combination of raw oysters, steamed clams, huge cooked shrimps, crabs, seasnails and other delicacies presented over a bed of ice in a large platter and decorated with lemon quarters and small containers of delicious sauces. It was accompanied by slices of rye bread and butter and a glass of white Loire Valley wine. At Isabelle's prompting, Catharine told more stories of her childhood during the war.

"We lived in Amsterdam during the war and had relatives in the country whom we often visited. They hid a little 'cousin' who was my age, but who, in reality, was a Jewish girl her parents had entrusted to them just before they were arrested. I loved Monica—that's the new name they had given her—I only found out what her real name was after the war. I became very close to her. She was quite sensitive and got sick a lot."

"What did your parents do?"

"My father was in the jewelry business and my mother did not work."

"Any brothers or sisters?"

"I had an older brother who died in the war." Catharine looked away. "After the war, Monica, whose parents died in a concentration camp, went to live in Israel with some distant relatives, and I came to America on a scholarship, to study at the University of Berkeley. That's about it. You know the "American Dream" part of my story."

Isabelle would have liked to know more: How her relatives managed to hide Monica without being caught. How it felt to live under the long German rule. What it was like to go to school during the war. How her parents obtained food and other goods. But Catharine did not elaborate and Isabelle did not want to push. Yet, it explained Catharine's need to face death so directly and even attach "beauty" to the reality.

"Are you still in touch with Monica?"

"I haven't heard from her in a long time. We kept in touch for a while, but you know how that goes. I think she's married and has children."

"What was her real name?"

"Rebecca. But I don't think she ever used it again. It was probably too hard for her to go back in time when her parents were gone forever. Anyway, Isabelle, let's talk about the present."

"I'd like to toast your ability to survive, Catharine."

They clicked glasses.

"This was the best dinner we've had in Paris yet," added Isabelle after sipping the last drop of her wine.

"We say that every night but it's true." Catharine looked at her watch. "Can you believe we've been here two hours? Can you imagine doing this in the States?"

"The only time I have dinner conversations like this is when I'm with my mother or you. It's truly an art. And now I know you so much better. I'd like to do this regularly when we get back. Maybe with some other friends, too."

"I'll try to make the *plateau de fruits de mer*."

"I'll make a raspberry tarte."

"People will knock down our doors to come to such a dinner."

"That's fine, as long as they contribute good conversation."

THEY PAID THE BILL and walked on to Saint Julien le Pauvre for the baroque music concert. Older than Notre Dame, the church was first built in 800, then rebuilt after it burned down. Isabelle liked the round Roman arches, the wood panels, the many precious icons and artifacts of orthodox faith. Beautiful candelabras glowed from above, casting a mysterious soft light on the knave, and the two women sat in the front, near the ensemble of Baroque instruments. They heard a Sonata in B minor by George Frederic Handel, performed on voice flute, positive organ, and bass viol, then a Sinfonia by Johann Sebastian Bach, performed on oboe d'amore, and finally the Pachelbel Kanon on alto recorder. The old instruments echoing through the ancient stones transported the women back to the Middle Ages.

The next day, Paris was on one of its many labor strikes that paralyze the whole city and most of France. "Nothing will be functioning," warned the concierge with the tattoos. "Not the Métro or busses or the post office, airlines, trains, garbage collections, schools, government buildings, everything will stop." She ticked off the dysfunctional entities on her fingers and then shook her hand in the air, a dozen bracelets rattling with emphasis. "Some stores will anticipate riots and terrorism. They'll pull down their iron curtains."

"How long will everything be closed," asked Catharine.

"It'll be chaos for a couple of days and then it will be like it never happened. The fun part is after dark when all the street people make music and dance. And then they storm the police barricades around the Palais du Justice. That's the best part of the protest."

"Can we go out on the streets?"

"No problem," said the young woman, rubbing mousse in her hair. "You'll just have to walk everywhere."

Isabelle and Catharine looked at each other and shrugged.

"I'm used to walking now," said Catharine.

Isabelle's Dream

Isabelle nodded. "I love it. Let's go find the Shakespeare and Company Bookshop. I bet it'll be open."

"We could browse while the skinheads storm the Bastille."

"I'll tell you about Sylvia Beach on the way."

The streets were full of disorganized congregations of people holding placards and banners. Isabelle led her friend past them on a pilgrimage to the namesake of the bookstore that Sylvia Beach, an American woman, ran in the early 1920s until it closed in 1941 during the Nazi occupation. Isabelle explained, "During its heyday it hosted some of the finest literary figures of the 20th century: Hemingway, Fitzgerald, Aragon, Dos Passos, Stein, Cummings, T.S Elliot, Gide. They all went to her lending library to read and critique each other's work. Sylvia even published the first edition of James Joyce's *Ulysses*. Apparently he left her in huge debt because she bankrolled his book. Then he went with a big publisher."

"Typical unappreciative man. But I wish I'd been a writer in those days," Catharine said.

"On the cutting edge. Talking about the deepest psychological revelations of the 20th century."

"I was thinking more about absinthe and free love."

"Take my picture, Catharine."

Isabelle posed in the doorway of the bookstore and then they went inside and browsed for a few hours. They treated themselves to lunch at the Brasserie Lipp on Saint-Germain Boulevard, a renowned restaurant, often frequented by stars and government officials. It was nearly empty because no officials were showing their faces during the strike. They tasted the best *choucroute garnie* Paris has to offer, a dish made of sauerkraut, boiled potatoes and an array of different sausages, ham, and other pork cuts. Strong mustard and a beer on tap were the accompaniments. To walk off the heavy but delicious meal, the two friends went to the terrace of the Café de Flore, one of Jean Paul Sartre's favorite hangouts during the heydays of Existentialism. Catharine looked at the menu and scowled. "Tea costs five dollars."

"Oh well, this is a historical café." Isabelle laughed. "I think we're probably paying for the spirits of Jean Paul Sartre and Simone de Beauvoir to have a cup of tea with us."

"I have never been much of a philosopher, and I don't know anything about Existentialism but its name. Tell me a little about it," Catharine asked hesitantly.

"In a nutshell, Existentialism started on the premise that 'existence' comes before 'essence.'"

"What does that mean?"

"Man is an accident of nature, not a creation in the image of God. And that it's through his life, his deeds, through throwing himself into his accidental existence, so to speak, and toiling in it, that he creates his own essence. He defines himself by what he does in his life and keeps on creating his essence until the day he dies, after which, there is nothing."

"And you think I'm gloomy with my interest in death."

"Nothingness is the word Jean-Paul Sartre uses. Basically, life is absurd, say the Existentialists, and meaning is only something Man creates for himself as he goes along."

"So, Jean-Paul Sartre did not believe in the spirit, the everlasting part of a person?"

"No. He was strictly an atheist. I often wonder whether he kept thinking this way when he was approaching his death, if his essence ever nagged at him then. It sure nags at me—more and more as I age. If he had acknowledged on his deathbed that he even considered spirituality, this would have negated his whole life's work. He could have never admitted it."

"It sounds almost simple. But what did this philosophy bring out that was an improvement for the human condition? Anything? I think you have to look death straight in the eye and acknowledge its power but also that it's… it's… it's just a brief passage and you go on into the next incarnation of your 'essence'."

"I guess it made people take more responsibility for their successes and failures in life."

"How so?"

"By defining the concept of freedom, for example. Existentialists feel that the only freedom humans can have in this life is that of commitment, so action becomes paramount. Like these workers in the streets today. Their behavior seems pointless to us but they are taking action for better labor conditions or benefits or safety or something like that."

Catharine yawned and stretched. "I see what you mean but I'll have to sleep on it. Right now, let's commit ourselves to going back to the hotel and writing a few post cards, shall we? I'm exhausted. This was a heavier day than my visits to the "cities of death," as you called them. Those Existentialists must have been so depressed all the time, with the burden of responsibility weighing on them like a yoke. One thing I know for sure, though, is that

I am not an Existentialist. My essence is alive and kicking, as well as the spirits of all these dead people I visited lately. I just know I've had an essence since I was born: the Essence of Catharine.

"I'm with you, Catharine, I believe in lightness and the light and things beyond our little life. But don't forget that this philosophy came straight out of the horrors of the last war. The world must have seemed quite absurd."

"I came out of that war, too, and I'm not a depressed existentialist."

"It's the strong *Essence de Catharine* that got you through."

"Hey, it's a new perfume!"

Isabelle took her friend's arm as they walked back to the hotel. Odd groups of protesters occasionally rushed past dragging dirty banners behind them. An older man passed them, muttering in disgust, "*Anarchistes.*" The rabble-rousers mostly seemed to be young men having a great time, skipping along, swigging from wine bottles, and bellowing protest slogans.

On the way back to the Scandinavian Hotel, they bought some cheese, some fresh fruit, a bottle of mineral water, and a crusty baguette to eat in the room. Isabelle patted the armored door statue and said, "*Bonne nuit.*" They clambered up the three flights to their room, wrote some postcards they'd picked up at Shakespeare and Company, and Catharine fell asleep early.

Isabelle could not go to sleep, though. She lay in bed quietly, but her mind and her heart wildly poured out ideas and feelings which blended into formless impressions, like a close-up of one of Monet's canvasses.

She felt a little depressed and let herself go, tossed between being and nothingness, summoning the only part of herself which could rescue her from sinking: her spirit. The events of the past few days had stirred her mind into a chaotic magma of Death, Beauty, Creativity, Life, War, Wit, and Freedom. The City of Light had thrown all these concepts at her with characteristic French irony and little connective tissue. Her thoughts swirled. France had always been at the vanguard of social and artistic ideas. Would a revolution ever come to pass here again? Was Catharine locked in her fascination with death? Were the Existentialists correct after all? Did Isabelle simply manufacture the idea of spirit, creating her own essence, programming it into her computer-mind as she had all of these other traits—teacher, daughter, lover, nature lover. These qualities that made her who she was? Where did her mind stop and her spirit start? She had always searched for wholeness, yet in this moment, she felt terribly fragmented, like the protesters on the street, disrupted but with nothing to pull together random truths.

Isabelle listened to the street noises coming in through the open window. Paris was still alive at two a.m. A gentle breeze lifted one of the curtains. Life was pulsing. Fields of energy had spirits of their own, like a river, and the whole universe flowed. Isabelle felt her cells blending with the great city outside her room. Maybe that was where the spirit was—simply in the flow. She abandoned herself to it, feeling the breeze, hearing the life, erasing all thoughts from her mind, and finally she fell into sleep, like a droplet into the river of time.

WHEN ISABELLE FINALLY WOKE UP at nine o' clock, Catharine was bustling about the room.

"You slept so well I didn't think you'd ever wake up. Here's your breakfast—a little cold, but ready. I'll call down for more hot coffee." Isabelle nodded and stretched out under the feather duvet.

Catharine dialed the room phone. "Please send a fresh cup of coffee to room #35. Really? That's good to know." Catharine raised her eyebrows. "Great. We'll be down soon. Yes, we just want more coffee."

She hung up and shook her head in amusement. "The concierge told me that the strikes will continue today, but by tomorrow, everything will go back to normal. She was such a brat. She even added, 'I told you that this would happen' with a triumphant tone in her voice."

"Just in time. Our train reservations are for tomorrow afternoon. I love Paris, but now I'm ready to get to my grandmother's place in the country. The city is beginning to frazzle me a little. I couldn't get to sleep."

"Why not?"

"I was thinking about Existentialism, everything we've seen. About you, too. The things you said about death and your games when you were a little girl. I realized that I really don't know much about your childhood, and it was intense."

Catharine waved off Isabelle's concern. "What are we going to do for our last day in Paris? I'd like to go deep down into history again, discover something more in this city's fascinating past."

Isabelle smiled. "We can't go very far if the Métro is still on strike." She grinned at her friend. "What ever happened to your plan to have a Parisian affair? I guess you'll have to hurry up if you want it to happen. Let's see, where could you start? Maybe a walk, by yourself, in the Luxembourg Garden?"

"I hate you, Isabelle. You are a complete rascal. Just wait, I might surprise you one of these days. Seriously, what do you want to do?"

"Let's ask the concierge. She's a brat but she knows the city."

After Isabelle had coffee and a shower, they went to the lobby. The concierge put down her nail file, delighted by the request to help. "There's a place, dear to my heart," she said with a twinkle in her eyes. "Walk to the Panthéon, it's not very far from here. There, just next to it, is L'Eglise Saint-Etienne Du Mont. Ask the little woman at the information table to tell you about the famous saint who lived in the fifth century, Saint Geneviève. It's a fascinating story of the Patroness of Paris. Makes me glad to be a Parisian… and a woman."

"Perfect," said Isabelle.

"Finally, some history about a woman," added Catharine.

They stepped into a gorgeous morning and walked happily along the route to the Panthéon. Lots of cars and taxis plugged the streets because of the public transportation strike. They passed Yasir's little Peugeot stuck in traffic on Boulevard Saint-Michel. His passenger was reading a newspaper in the back. Yasir waved at the women and then suddenly jumped out of the taxi and ran toward them.

"Oh, oh," whispered Catharine.

"American women! American women, I must tell you," he shouted as he leapt up the curb and practically danced around them. "I go to Libya next week. My wife she is so happy."

"Wonderful, Yasir, wonderful." Isabelle laughed as he waved goodbye, raced back to his cab, and jumped in just as traffic began to move forward. His passenger never looked up from his paper.

Catharine looked at her friend, shaking her head in disbelief. "And I thought he'd accost us on a dark and stormy night. The *Essence d'Isabelle* prevailed. I'm impressed."

"Catch more flies with honey, my stepfather used to say." And Isabelle cast a silent greeting out to David Chalmers.

They passed the formidable domed Panthéon but decided that they'd visit it later and headed directly for Saint-Etienne Du Mont.

They entered the church under its stunning rose window and stood speechless. They had never seen the high gallery called a jube. Two spiraling staircases wrapped around pillars on each side of the nave and then rejoined forming a high bridge that was a special place for prayer. The jube was made of stone but it looked as if it was made of lace. Light, reflected through the stained glass windows, played on the staircases in shimmering, otherworldly dots. Isabelle and Catharine walked around the church into the small chapel dedicated to Saint Geneviève. There were hundreds of burning candles and several people knelt in silence.

They followed signs to an information table and Isabelle asked the chapel caretaker, "Why are there so many worshipers today."

The woman's face lit up, but she replied in a very soft voice, "Come, we'll go to the visitors' room." The tiny woman stood and led them to a small room in back of the chapel with a large wooden door that dwarfed her five-foot frame. Nonetheless, she closed it softly behind them so it wouldn't reverberate through the church. She sat at a table and gestured her guests to the other chairs. With a warm smile, she greeted them. "*Bienvenue*, my name is Beatrice. We will not be disturbed in here. To answer your question: there are so many people today in the chapel because there is this trouble in Paris. People come here to pray to Saint Geneviève: they feel that she can help. She once saved the city and she has watched over Paris ever since." The woman's voice filled with pride and she straightened her shoulders. "They tried to destroy her memory during the revolution, but they could not even do that because she was a very strong woman and strong women never die."

Beatrice paused and looked at her guests. "Would you like to hear the whole story?"

"Of course," said Catharine with a quick glance at Isabelle, who nodded in agreement. Isabelle was still enraptured from the candlelight and now from the inexplicable sway of this small woman.

"*Eh bien*," said Beatrice, and she sat back, relaxed, and began to speak with the cadence and practice of a natural storyteller. "Geneviève was born in 420 and died in 512. She was a woman famous for her gift of healing and accomplishing miracles. Extremely devoted to the Christian faith, she prayed a lot and took care of poor people, distributing bread, helping to care for them during epidemics, floods, fires, and other scourges. Geneviève was a being of light! Have you ever met such a being?"

"Yes," said Catharine, "My friend Monica… during the war."

"Ah yes. War has a way of bringing both the darkest and the lightest out of people. Paris was just a small island, then, surrounded by gates that could be closed in case of an enemy attack. In 451, Attila the Hun—a truly dark human being—came all the way from the high plateaus of Central Asia, ravaging everything on his way. It was said that where Attila passed through, the grass wouldn't grow back again. His soldiers were bloody mercenaries who pillaged, raped, massacred, and burned everything they encountered. They were much worse than the wild wolves which threatened

Isabelle's Dream

the countryside. Attila eventually arrived in sight of Paris. His savages were now encamped one hour by horseback from the city. The town crier called all of the Parisians in, and the gates to the city were closed. Attila intended to crown his conquest by looting the many treasures of Paris; He sent an ultimatum to the citizens saying that unless the Parisians handed over all the treasures and opened the gates, every person and animal would be tortured and massacred and the city would be reduced to ashes. The city fathers feared the worst. In desperation, they consulted Geneviève who prayed and reflected and declared that she would go and speak to Attila. She insisted that she did not need any escort.

"Geneviève departed through the gates of Paris on horseback and rode to Attila's camp. The savages were completely flabbergasted to see this young woman, alone, requesting to speak to the chief, but she had such a presence that they took her to meet him. It is a mystery to this day what she said in the famous encounter. The legend says the meeting lasted several hours, but as a result, Attila and his warriors left without attacking Paris. Attila headed back east and, the story goes, while the army was crossing a river, all were engulfed in the icy waters and his treasures were lost. No one knows if this is true, but the part about Paris being saved by the young woman is indeed authentic. And this is how Geneviève, soon to be canonized, became the Patroness of Paris, the city she has protected ever since."

Neither Catharine nor Isabelle said anything at first; they were so entranced by the mesmerizing voice of Beatrice. Finally, Isabelle shook her head a little. "What a truly amazing story. Thank you so much for telling it to us." She began to rise out of her seat.

Beatrice put up her hand. "But wait, it is not over yet. A church was built in Saint Geneviève's honor and her sarcophagus placed in the church after she died. People continued to come and pray to her for a long time. When the revolution came, in 1789, the church was destroyed. The revolutionaries felt that Geneviève had power—probably as a symbol of the dominance of the Catholic Church—and they wanted to destroy it. They stormed the church and hauled Saint Geneviève's sarcophagus to the Seine and threw it in the water. Some of the relics were saved, though, and the Panthéon was later built on the location of the former church, intended to honor Saint Geneviève again. However, in 1791, the Panthéon became a temple destined to shelter the ashes of great Frenchmen, so now we have all of these famous guys there—Voltaire, Victor Hugo, Rousseau, Zola, Braille. And it has become a temple to the glory of many great men instead of one brave woman. Saint Geneviève has been relegated to this small chapel."

Beatrice sighed and then got a mischievous look in her eye. She leaned forward and whispered, "But did you see how popular she still is? Just count the candles. Incredible, isn't?"

"I would like to light a candle in the chapel," said Catharine. Beatrice handed them each a votive and opened the great doors. Isabelle and Catharine added their small candles to the sea of flickering light and stayed for a while in the chapel, sitting quietly, praying for solace in difficult times with the many people of Paris.

When they reentered the streets, blinking in the bright sunlight, they decided not to stop at the Panthéon after all. Their loyalties were with the single woman saint who saved the City of Lights.

"Spirit triumphed over brute force. That's the core of Geneviève's story in spite of the desecration of the church."

"Where are the Genevièves of today's world?" wondered Isabelle. "Women have always been the peacemakers, ever counterbalancing the negative.

"You know, Isabelle, with Geneviève and Jeanne d'Arc, France has two mighty heroines in her past. Is there something different about the idea of Woman in the French psyche?"

"I think so, but it's difficult to put it into words. There's a certain veneration of women, perhaps?"

"Women may have a little more prestige here. It is a subtle feeling, but I can sense it."

"I hope I can hold on to that strength and take some home with me."

Isabelle and Catharine walked back to their hotel and rested for a while. Then they headed to the restaurant they had selected for their farewell dinner in Paris: La Closerie Des Lilas. Located on top of Saint-Michel Boulevard, near the Observatory, it was a classic French restaurant with a view on the Jardin du Luxembourg. It had a 1930s decor. Less sophisticated than Maxim's, but with more charm, it was an island of peace. The cuisine was typically French. Catharine decided to ask the Maitre d'Hôtel for his advice, adding that they were celebrating their last evening in Paris and wanted to eat a deeply authentic French dinner. "Count on me, mes dames," he said with a flourish.

He first brought some *asperges vinaigrette*, the white variety, which tasted so tender. Next was *un gigot aux flageolets*, slices of leg of lamb cut at their table and served with fresh beans and a green salad, and finally a dessert to die for: *profiterolles au chocolat*, a heavenly chocolate pastry. Isabelle leaned back and closed her eyes as she lingered on a bite. "There is no way to describe this in English, they agreed. They ordered a Médoc 86 to drink with their meal, a Bordeaux wine, which went down like velvet and warmed their bodies as well as their souls. The restaurant's atmosphere was quietly elegant. And the friends reminisced happily about all of their adventures, drank to the good life and to all the Genevièves of the world. "And to the perfect meal to end the most wonderful six days," toasted Catharine.

While walking back by the Luxembourg Garden, a full moon rose above the city and their trust in the magic of Paris was fulfilled.

In the morning, standing next to their luggage in front of the Scandinavia Hotel, Catharine and Isabelle hugged and said their goodbyes before leaving in two different directions. Catharine would catch her train to Amsterdam at the Gare du Nord and Isabelle her train to Lyon at the Gare de Lyon. They had shared much intimacy but their banter was playfully light.

"We'll see each other next in about three weeks. You be careful, now, in Amsterdam. No crazy affair that would cause you to miss our flight. I am counting on you, Catharine."

"And what about you, Miss Romantic? You know how the French men are. You handle the language so well, I wouldn't be surprised if one mesmerizes you with his charming *Rs*. Seriously, though, have a great time with your grandmother. I know what this time means to you."

"And you are revisiting a difficult time in your past. The time has come to plunge into our ancestry!"

"I only wish there were some more Genevièves in the lot, or maybe a Monet or a Gide. More likely it'll be some of those undistinguished skeletons, like the ones we saw in the Catacombs."

"We'll have a lot to talk about when we meet on Air France Flight #22."

They heard a wild honking horn and turned. "Oh, oh," said Catharine with a laugh. "It's our good friend Yasir in his Peugeot."

IV

The Forest

Isabelle took a taxi to the Gare de Lyon and arrived early for her one o'clock departure on the *train à grande vitesse*, or high-speed train. She wandered aimlessly around the giant clock in the center of the station, feeling a little strange, almost sad. She dismissed the idea that she could be upset to find herself alone after having had such a great time with Catharine. Of course, she missed her friend, but no, that wasn't it. In spite of the strike, all had gone so well in Paris for the two women. Now Catharine was heading north and she was going south.

It was important that she be alone; there was something significant that she had come to do in this country, even though it was a venture into the unknown, perhaps into the mirror in the field of her dream. As she strolled through the busy crowd, she caught the fringes of conversations in her language of origin. "*Vite, vite!*" "*Je suis désolé.*" "*Non, non, Maman.*" A small child suddenly bumped into her knees and made her stagger. "*Pardon, madame,*" said the boy cheerfully, and Isabelle snapped out of her reverie. "Enough aimless meandering. It's dangerous," she chastised herself with a grin and headed for the Buffet de la Gare for a café au lait while waiting for her train.

Soon she was sitting in her reserved window seat. The TGV would take her from Paris to Lyon in two short hours, an incredible feat. A flight between the two cities took at least three hours, counting the trips to and from both airports. The last time, Isabelle had made the trip to Lyon with George on the regular train, and it had taken them five hours. He had snored the whole way. It was puzzling that she had found his California getaways so enticing and romantic, yet whenever they traveled beyond their few weekend retreats, he seemed so uninspired, so unimaginative, so lacking in the pleasure of new sights.

The train started slowly at first. When it passed the last suburban areas, it sped into the rolling countryside. Isabelle abandoned herself to its movement as it accelerated on and on, faster and faster. She felt like an astronaut being launched into space, giving total trust to the vehicle and the journey. Her seat felt like a delicious cocoon and she snuggled down into it. The repetitive noise of the wheels on the tracks lulled her into a hypnotic state. Fields rolled by, small farms, trees, a hill here and there, deep forest in the distance. All this happening outside of myself, she thought. And who am I in the midst of it all?

As Isabelle asked that question, closing her eyes, she felt transported into an odd state, as if she had expanded into one of those forests that paraded outside her window, except that the landscape was immaterial. "Peace" was the only way to describe the sensation. Although these forests of peace were outside of herself, so visual and full of motion, she felt their essence reside deep in her body.

Isabelle flashed back on her discussion with Catharine about Existentialism and realized that she had merely paid lip service to explaining the philosophy to her friend without completely understanding its opposite. What did Essence really mean? An underlying realm of the self? Like the place beyond the forest's edge? Was it the dimension beyond one's body? Is that what the soul was all about? She could feel something hazy, ineffable. She opened her eyes and took in the green flowing countryside again, feeling deeply settled, seeing her gently smiling face reflected back at her from the window as if she were merged with the landscape. She abandoned herself to the sensation and it remained with her till she reached Lyon.

The "reality" of existence resumed when the train came to a stop at the platform. As she picked up her belongings, bumping elbows with other passengers, she thought, I tripped out, as the hippies used to say. The flower children sought Nirvana with gurus, at ashrams, on mountaintops, and in sweat lodges. Now it had happened to her, briefly, on the TGV, of all places.

Isabelle caught her connection to La Tour du Pin in Lyon. The train was a slower model. Still under the spell of the TGV, Isabelle thought about what awaited her in La Bâtie: her grandmother, her intention to elucidate her dream by searching the family background, to find out some of the reasons for her problem with men and lack of sense of purpose. All these pragmatic concerns compared very little with the brief but intense experience of bliss. Her human problems didn't fit in with this other dimension in herself. She felt puzzled as the little towns kept passing before her eyes. She blew a quick breath out between pursed lips. So much self-examination ahead. Such high expectations for revelations and change. But, wait, maybe something big did happen within that forest of peace. Maybe she could trust her experience. Was this a place she could always go into at the core of her being, and see her own smile, just like she smiled at the train window and the mirror in her dream? Yes, she had gotten her first clue.

She suddenly felt tired and hungry, and that is never helpful when looking for big answers.

Isabelle thought of California, where the slopes of Mount Diablo are completely brown at this time of the year, and she wondered whether Marguerite had experienced a certain shock when she had first moved to the Golden State. Another train thundered by on the next track. Speed, she thought, ever increasing speed. Her ancestors had made the same trip by foot once, exposed to the elements and every obstacle of nature. Did they enjoy it more? It took the ones who rode in coaches one week to reach the same destination. In the early days of train travel, it became one day. Isabelle thought of the Myth of Sisyphus, as described by Camus, and how Sisyphus was compelled to push his rock up the hill, finding odd solace in the act, knowing full well that the rock would tumble back down as soon as it reached the top. But he continued to push on. It was a gloomy image of the human condition. Had man merely devised ways to push faster and faster, increasing the speed of the rock? Wouldn't happiness more likely come from accepting that this was the human plight, to look at it with a grin, from the top of the hill, and then, knowingly, keep pushing one's chosen rock on one's chosen path, rather than inventing always faster and better means of distracting oneself into an endless illusion that the effort matters. Isabelle smiled as she thought of her path. This trip was part of it, slowly or at high speed, she was moving. She closed her eyes, cleared her mind of all thoughts, and let herself be carried up the Sisyphian hill.

At La Tour Du Pin she got off the train, put her small backpack on, pulling her light rolling suitcase behind her. She immediately recognized the old-fashioned train station, almost unchanged since her last visit, except for the addition of a coffee shop next to it. Located in the foothills of the Alps, the country beyond the station was bursting with vivid hues, burgeoning, blooming, sprouting into fat fields and vegetable gardens.

Isabelle caught a bus to her grandmother's village, La Bâtie Montgascon—the last leg of her journey. It came to a stop where it always had, in front of a café across from the central fountain. Leaving her suitcase at the café, where it could be picked up later, she started to walk toward her grandmother's house. The air was completely familiar as she started the long climb along the woods up the hill. One of the few weaving factories left in the village beat its rhythmic melody of shuttles, raddles, and spools into the street. Why did she think of a cat, all of a sudden? Oh, yes! Her grandmother's neighbor who ran the small mill let her cat run around the weaving machines and play with the scraps of fabric. Isabelle used to love to visit the orange tiger cat and the sound of the machines made her think of her furry friend.

One turn in the road and Isabelle found herself in front of the place where she walked with her grandmother to buy eggs. She remembered the feeling of her grandmother's hand pulling her away to return home because it was time to make dinner. Her grandmother was always on time.

There were new unfamiliar houses along the road. Why do things have to change so much, she thought, especially since I need to look to the past. Isabelle hastened her pace when she passed by the farmhouse where the neighbors had raised goats to make cheese. Another few yards and she was in the middle of a stately park where her grandmother Claire's house rested amongst the trees, just as she remembered it. The trees had grown so much that it resembled a forest now, with pines and linden trees, a blue spruce in the middle of the meadow, the cherry tree she'd picked fruit from, now old and gnarly. Closer to the house was the small chicken coop now transformed into a garage, it seemed. A garage? Where were her grandfather's chickens and rabbits?

Isabelle turned down an alley shaded by chestnut trees and finally saw the solid old two-story house. She stopped at the wooden gate with the original wooden latch and absorbed the scene of many childhood memories. The house was muted white stucco with a steep slate roof. An amusing steeple stuck up like an exhaust pipe over the kitchen, and under the gable, there was a little oval attic window covered with a board painted red brown, inviting the mystery of what might lie behind the covered glass. The rest of the windows were long and narrow with metal shutters. They cast a dim cool light into the house that was the backlight for all Isabelle's dreams. Isabelle lifted the latch and the gate opened with a loud squeak.

Immediately, the heavy dark red front door opened with a thwack. A woman rushed out and ran to meet her. "You must be Isabelle," she said in English with a rich French accent. She reached for Isabelle's hand, both shaking it in greeting and pulling her along the path to the house with effusive energy. "I am Mademoiselle Michaut, your grandmother's housekeeper-nurse-occasional gardener-handy woman, and anything else she needs." She laughed. "And shoulder to cry on—although your grandmother is not one to cry easily, as you know."

"And how is my grandmother?" Isabelle asked, pausing to get her arms out of her backpack before they entered the house.

"Well, you'll see. Pretty good for her age, I would say. She eats like a horse, sleeps like a baby, complains most of the time and keeps me running around. She can be wonderful and sweet, at times, but *elle est impossible, je vous dis*. Impossible." Mademoiselle Michaut punctuated her description by lifting her arms up in the air, the palms of her hands wide open with the playful inevitability of the situation.

Isabelle shook her head and smiled. She walked into the living room where Claire, all dressed in black, was sitting in her wheel chair, next to the window. She pointed a gnarled finger at Mademoiselle Michaut. "I heard you call me impossible."

"I was just testing your hearing, which I see is quite fine." Mademoiselle Michaut backed gracefully out of the living room adding, "Enjoy your granddaughter. I'll be in the kitchen."

Two large dark eyes stared at Isabelle out of an emaciated bony face. "Well, well, if it isn't my little American granddaughter. Come here, long lost child, and let me take a look at you."

Isabelle kissed her grandmother's gaunt cheek affectionately, smelling the strong scent of camphor that Mamie had always touted as a panacea for every disease. For the most part, it seemed to have worked. Except for more wrinkles, the loss of a few pounds, and this wheelchair she was sitting in, Claire was the same intense woman she remembered so well. Her hair was tied in a bun behind her head, as always, and a velvet ribbon adorned her neck. Marguerite had once told her that Mamie's ever-present ribbon was a vanity to conceal her dropping chin. Her grandmother wouldn't be able to chase Isabelle up the stairs, like she did when Isabelle was a little girl. She probably could not cook those wonderful meals anymore. Hopefully she also muted her sharp criticism of neighbors and family members, but her eyes seemed as crisp and clear as they always had been.

"I am so happy to see you, Mamie. You look great."

"Great? Ah, you don't know about my terrible arthritis then. It is not fun getting old, I'm telling you. I can't see well anymore, I forget everything, I spend hours awake at night, I hate to be stuck in this contraption of a chair, and..."

"But as Mademoiselle Michaut says, you hear like a fox."

Mamie looked at her askance with a little grin. "I see already I'll get no sympathy from you. Just like your mother. How is Marguerite? She's no spring chicken herself."

Isabelle grinned at the familiar irascible tongue of her stern grandmother. It had been upsetting at times but she'd learned to hear the undertone of affection. "Mother is fine and she sends her love. She enjoys working in her antique store. She'll be here in the fall."

"If I'm still around, that is."

"Mamie, you said the same thing when I visited you the last time. It's been three years and you're still here."

"Yes, I remember. You came by with your husband. What was his name? Bill?"

"George. And he wasn't my husband."

Mamie waved a dismissive hand. "You modern women. A nice fellow. I liked him."

"He could be charming when he wanted to." Isabelle looked away. "Anyway, he's not in my life now."

"Why haven't you married, Isabelle? Of course, everybody is getting divorced these days, so maybe it's for the best." Claire rested her head against the back of her chair as if it was all too much to take. "But you didn't stay very long the last time, just a couple of days. I hope you'll stay longer this time."

"I'm here for a few weeks, if that's okay. You'll probably get weary of me after you find out all the questions I have for you. I'm on a family quest. That's why Marguerite sent me. She couldn't answer all my annoying questions."

"Not too many Isabelle, please. I really don't remember anything. Let's go to the dining room now. Eating is one of the only pleasures in life that I still can enjoy. Mademoiselle Michaut made a special supper in your honor." Isabelle pushed Mamie's wheelchair down the hall through the dim evening light. Mademoiselle Michaut turned on the lights and waved them into the dining room filled with the scent of a warm, freshly prepared meal. Isabelle felt enveloped in French herbs.

At the table, Isabelle watched with amazement how her grandmother wolfed down her vegetable soup, chicken quiche, green salad, and fruit compote topped with a cookie, all accompanied by sips from a quarter of a glass of red wine. The portions were all small, but Isabelle thought, What a hardy woman, a force of nature Mamie is. A side dish of green beans brought back the image of her grandfather tying the bean stalks to the trestle. From spring to fall his garden offered something fresh and delectable for the table.

Mamie wiped her lips with the linen napkin and sighed with contentment. "It is almost my bed time, now. I retire early these days," she declared, looking at the ancient clock leaning against the wall. "Eight o'clock will strike soon." And it did strike, just then, with a flat deep metallic tone. Isabelle remembered her grandfather, up on a chair, winding the clock. She remembered him putting his dentures on the table before he started winding the clock, inviting a grimace from his wife. The women in the household used to tease him when he had his dentures out and make him repeat difficult words. But he had a great sense of humor about it, lisping and smiling behind his beard. Why he couldn't wind the clock with his dentures in, she never knew.

Across from the clock, the old piano stood against the wall under a picture of Chopin playing his last piece as he is dying, with his white long hands on the keyboard. Everything was in the same place as it was when she visited years ago except her grandfather's presence. Isabelle felt a quick sting of loss.

Mamie pushed the wheels of her chair back from the table, and Mademoiselle Michaut instantly appeared from the kitchen to push her down the hall to help the old woman with her bedtime preparations. "Sleep well, Isabelle," Mamie said with sleepy warmth. "Mademoiselle Michaut prepared your Aunt Justine's room for you upstairs, the one you stayed in with Bill, I mean George. It has the best view on the park. I sleep downstairs, myself, nowadays." She grinned back at her granddaughter and added, "For obvious reasons."

Isabelle followed them, and before they turned in Mamie's bedroom, she kissed her grandmother loudly on both cheeks. "Good night, Mamie. We'll talk tomorrow."

It was still light outside. Isabelle stepped out the thick wooden door and wandered through the park for an evening walk. She marveled at the size of the trees, some of which seemed twice as big since her last trip. The cherry tree still had a few ripe cherries on one of its branches; she reached for two whose stems were attached together, just like the ones she would hang from her ears like earrings when she was a little girl. She passed by the old barn, now empty, where her grandfather kept his rabbits. Once, when she was four, she had discovered a litter of kittens hidden in the hay and screamed with delight. As she walked around, many of her other childhood memories slipped back, and seeing herself once again as a carefree child warmed her heart in the balmy June evening. Her grandfather's image walked with her through the dusk, wearing his casual gardening clothes. His garden was his joy and he offered baskets full of every kind of vegetable and the most delicious strawberries. Isabelle had loved to snatch some before they made it to the kitchen and then snuggle in his arms. Even now, his presence was comforting and sweet. She smelled his earthy scent.

The mountains slowly darkened in the distance. Isabelle sat on a lounge chair under the linden tree, remembering the family gatherings in that very place. Weariness from the long day of travel crept over her as night fell. She stood and took one last deep breath, walked to the front door and pulled on the big copper handle she once couldn't even reach.

The dim wooden staircase creaked as she ascended to the second-floor rooms. Isabelle collapsed in Aunt Justine's bed, exhausted and the magic sounds of this lovely night, coming through a window opened wide on the park, soon put Isabelle into a deep sleep.

She woke up around five, laughing so hard that she could not stop for minutes. In her dream there was a steep green hill, in a place that resembled some of the landscapes she had seen the day before through the train window. George was at the foot of the hill, with a large rock in front of him. He was dressed in a loincloth, and he looked very strange because he had a full beard and no other clothes on. He started to push the rock up the hill, with great effort and a painful facial expression. Isabelle saw her dream-self sitting on top of the hill with Catharine. When George got to the middle of the hill, Isabelle yelled to him "Why don't you just stop and smell the roses?" Catharine added, "And smell the strawberries, the vegetables and the Mona Lisa, too." But George unhappily continued pushing the rock as if he had not heard them. Isabelle and her friend started laughing again—and then Isabelle woke up, in a fit of giggles.

Isabelle rolled on her side and looked through the tall window. The light gray of dawn slowly backlit the trees in the park. She began to feel a little guilty about her heartless dream. Poor George struggled so painfully with the rock. Was her dream trying to show her how insensitive she had been toward him? The daylight rose in her room along with the realization that she was in France, already claiming a life far beyond the petty grievances of petulant, inebriated George. The symbolism behind the comic scene of her dream became pretty obvious, and this time, she did not need her psychology teacher to help her with the clues. She had envisioned George as Sisyphus pushing his rock—his addiction—in a relentless way, unwilling to listen to the women telling him to stop and smell all the true things in life. The women had laughed because they were looking at the situation from the top of the hill, and they were smug about it. That's the part Isabelle didn't liked very much. Instead of being smug, maybe she could be more charitable toward George from now on. She closed her eyes, trying to send loving thoughts to him. But he was too funny, dressed in a loincloth with his long beard, Catharine telling him to "smell" the Mona Lisa. Isabelle drew her covers over her face to smother another snicker. Dreams were simply out of control. If it was funny, she had to laugh. If it was disturbing, like her big snake dream, a dream could change the course of your life. After all that's why she was lying in this bed in La Bâtie following strange clues to her family history and herself. She was carrying her own rock up the hill as well. Unlike George, though, she stopped to smell the flowers once

Isabelle's Dream

in a while. Still, there was no reason to be smug about it—unless, she was also laughing at herself and her clumsy attempts at growing. Aren't all the characters in a dream only parts of oneself anyway?

Imagining again the row of stern women in black reflected in her dream mirror, Isabelle almost drifted back to sleep. But below the floorboards, she heard pots rattling in the kitchen and Claire's wheelchair maneuvering toward the dining room. She hopped out of bed and ran down the old stairs in her pajamas. Her first big day of discovery was about to begin, and Grandmother was a stickler about getting to meals on time.

𝒱

Grandmother

"**G**ood morning, Mamie. Did you sleep well?" Isabelle kissed her grandmother on the cheek and slipped into her chair. "Good morning, Mademoiselle." Mademoiselle smiled at Isabelle while pouring Claire a large bowl of café au lait.

"I had a terrible night, as usual," grumbled Claire reaching for a piece of bread from a basket on the table. "The neighbor's dog kept barking. Why do these people keep that horrible mutt? Did you hear the beast, Isabelle?"

"No, I slept wonderfully well and I woke up laughing. I had the window opened all night and I heard the crickets but not the dog."

"It's market day. I'll drive your grandmother to the village, today. Do you want to join us?" asked Mademoiselle from the kitchen doorway.

"No, thank you. I'd prefer to take a walk to the river, but could you bring my suitcase back? I left it at the café yesterday, the one by the bus stop. I forgot all about it."

"What in the world are you going to the river for?" Claire grumbled. "There are snakes in the bushes and the mill is abandoned. The road is bad, all rocky. It hasn't been kept in ages."

"Just something I want to do, Mamie. Don't worry. When you get back, we'll have a nice visit. I want to ask you something about snakes."

"Hew, terrible creatures. I hate them."

Mademoiselle sat down next to Isabelle and the three women ate their breakfast while listening to the news on the radio of a farmers' protest in Paris: "More than 3,000 French farmers demonstrated in Paris on Wednesday, protesting the liberalization of the European Union's cereal, beef, and dairy sectors."

"Bah!" exclaimed Claire, "Those farmers are just looking for a lot of attention."

"What are they protesting, Mamie?" asked Isabelle.

"They want more money, as always, with no thought to the rest of us just trying to buy a few groceries."

Mademoiselle cleared her throat as she poured Claire more coffee. "They don't want to *lower* their prices just because Americans want cheap food. I like good local products. The more French, the better."

Claire waved her hand. "But why do these people keep on striking all the time? Messing up streets and stopping everyone's life. It just makes everybody angry."

"There was a labor strike in Paris when I was there three days ago. The buses and trains shut down but I didn't actually mind walking around the city. And by nightfall it was just a few anarchists running around the streets."

Claire clicked her coffee cup loudly on its saucer. "You were lucky your train ran yesterday, Isabelle, very lucky. I'm telling you, it's a pity things are getting worse in this. Thank God, I won't have to put up with all that trouble too much longer." Claire took a bite of bread. She looked at Isabelle who looked at Mademoiselle Michaut who winked back. Neither one said anything. Claire sighed her disappointment loudly, pushed her chair away from the table, and wheeled toward her room.

LA LEYSSE RIVER HELD A SPECIAL PLACE in Isabelle's heart. She hadn't been able to walk around when she was here with George, three years ago. They'd been too busy driving around the areas he wanted to explore, especially a couple of ski resorts he had heard about. And George drove worse than the French on the little winding roads. He always had an open bottle of wine, too, exclaiming as he took a swig, "Wine any time of day just like the French."

Isabelle pushed aside the bushes that enshrouded the banks of the river and put her hand in the cool water. She had gone fishing there, with her grandfather, and later they looked for mushrooms in the woods. While holding his large rugged hand, everything had seemed possible and magical. Even if the snakes crossed their path, Isabelle thought and chuckled. He had warned her with exaggerated seriousness, his thick eyebrows low over his blue eyes, to watch out for snakes but they had never seen even one.

The woods behind her were humid and dim. The river wound away and disappeared in a curve. When she fished with her grandfather, sometimes another fisherman emerged silently around the bend, walking in high boots and carrying a basket for his catch. He tossed his line into the water again and again as if there was no one else in the world but himself and the elusive trout. Like a meditation she thought, recollecting the serene image.

Isabelle tossed a stone into the water and headed back to the trail that led to a wooden water wheel up a fork in the river. She walked steadily and deliberately, noticing the willow branches arching above her as if she were on a passage, a pilgrimage. The shady path was as beautiful as ever, smelling of fresh mint and beds of decaying leaves. Isabelle touched, smelled, and wondered, reminding herself what she once did in a this spot or that spot, recognizing a special tree or a timeworn cottage. Every memory filled her with energy until she was almost skipping along like a little girl.

She reached the fork but it was just a dry overgrown gulley. She walked beside it up over a small rise, the calm penetrated by the disquieting noise of cars. She stiffened in anticipation. There, on the other side of an old bridge, was an embankment that had been built to support the highway. Above it, the traffic flowed like blood from a swollen wound. Isabelle stood in disbelief, picturing the beautiful woods and fields that had once surrounded the river and its forks. The freeway was a barrier arresting her memories and all their exquisite sensations. Isabelle gasped. The true landscape had been raped and plundered.

She continued on. Nettles had invaded the dried up river branch where the water wheel once stood, ivy and debris covered the bridge rail she used to lean on when fishing with her grandfather. The house next to it was in ruins and the barnyard silent; only birds flitted above and lizards ran along the cracks in the walls. The grass was high and lush, the nettles enormous, thriving in their newfound bed. Isabelle brushed against them and swallowed her sobs as they stung her forearm. She ran all the way back to the river, dunked her stinging skin in the cool water, and silently came back to the present. There was no way to find her youth. She had come to reclaim some sense of her youth but the place of her recollections had been brutally bulldozed. She glanced right and left for other memories to hang on to, some unchanged place to reassure her fears. The beautiful memories of the water wheel and the river were no more, torn apart like the pristine joy of her childhood, and it hurt.

Isabelle strode back along the path to the house and up to her room. She threw herself on the bed, pulling in great gulps of air. After a while, a gentle voice rose above the bitter noise in her mind. "Isabelle, life goes on. Let go; let go. Your memories will always be there for you." Isabelle felt a few tears fall down her cheeks, and then she sat up to look at the nettle's light pink welt on her arm, which no longer hurt. She got up to get a tissue and saw a small picture of Pépé on the wall by the door. He was holding his garden trowel and smiling. She remembered him talking about nettles. "Isabelle," he had said to her while she itched furiously where a nettle had scraped her arm, "nettles sting you to wake you up. They are the first plants to return after the land has been disturbed. They are the survivors. This will hurt for a minute and then you will feel very good, you'll see." And he had been right. Then and now.

CLAIRE AND FLORENCE RETURNED from the market with bags full of fresh vegetables, milk, cheese, and meat from the butcher as well as her suitcase. Claire grumbled about the crowds in town and rolled off to her room for a nap. Isabelle took her suitcase upstairs and started to put things away. Mademoiselle Michaut followed her to help tidy up the room.

"Can I call you by your first name, Mademoiselle? I know people are very formal in France when they don't know a person well, but… "

"Yes, yes, call me Florence and I'll call you Isabelle, okay?"

Isabelle nodded. "You know, I think that I am starting to see what you mean about my grandmother being impossible. Did she behave at the market?"

"So-so. She kept calling to people through the car window to tell them that her granddaughter the American was in town but that you had to go to the river right away for some reason. She also had me return the green beans because they were too stringy." Florence grinned. "That's nothing unusual."

"Claire is quite a character! I'll sit with her in the garden, this afternoon. You can get a break."

After lunch, Claire took a short nap. At three o' clock, Florence helped her outside to a shady place under the linden tree. Isabelle was already there, trying to read Colette's *Claudine à Paris* in French.

"Did you have a good rest, Mamie? You look refreshed."

"Not too bad. I seem to rest better during the day. Tell me, Isabelle, what did you go to the river for? What was so urgent?"

"I just wanted to see the place where I went fishing with Pépé when I was four years old. Mamie, there's a freeway there. I was so shocked."

"I thought you knew it. They built it at least ten years ago. I haven't seen the place, myself. I refuse to go there. Did you see any snakes, Isabelle?"

"What is that fascination that you have with snakes, Mamie? No, I did not see a single one and I never have."

"There are vipers in the bushes at the river, I'm telling you. Someone from the village got stung by a big one, a long time ago, and died. I always warned your mother about snakes when she was little."

"Yes, Mother told me. She remembers it well."

Claire looked at her askance. "What else did she tell you about me?"

"That you were a strong woman, that you pulled the family through during the war with your determination."

"Yes. We all did our best, though." Mamie shrugged her little shoulders. "Nothing unusual. But your mother had to get married to that resistance fighter father of yours. He was doing some dangerous stuff, and I had warned her and warned her about it but she didn't listen. Headstrong girl from the day she was born. She couldn't wait to get married—but I was right. He got shot, of course, taking some refugees to the docks. That didn't stop Marguerite, though. After the war she eloped with an American," she put her hand to her chest, "taking our only granddaughter away, abandoning her own country." Isabelle thought Claire looked very relaxed back in her chair, her body language quite different from the tone of condemnation and tragedy.

"We weren't very happy about that either. At least I have *one* daughter who stayed in France."

"Aunt Germaine. I guess I feel we all have our destinies, Mamie. I'm happy Mother decided to marry David. He was a great dad and I loved him a lot." Mamie scowled and was about to say something but Isabelle handed her a package wrapped in tissue. "Oh, I forgot, here, look what she knitted for you."

Mamie pulled open the paper and spread out a handmade beige and white wrap. Claire looked at it, carefully examining all the different stitches with long thin fingers, turning it over several times. She rubbed it on her cheek. "*Merveilleux*, Marguerite has always been very good with her hands. She did a wonderful job. You will thank her for me."

"You can tell her yourself. She'll be here in a few weeks."

Mamie looked confused and then sighed. "Ah, yes, I remember now." She stroked the gift and drew it around her shoulders. "Now, with Germaine, it was different. She was better with her brain. She went to college and became a pharmacist, you know."

"I know, Mamie, but Mother is not so bad with her brain, either. You should see how well she runs her antique shop! No need to compare the two."

"Competition, Isabelle. Competition makes people want to surpass themselves. Germaine and Marguerite did a lot of that in school, and it helped them both get good grades."

"I don't think that Mother liked it, really." Isabelle thought, *And why do you think Mother got married so young and then went to America?* but she didn't want to hurt the old woman. Instead, she said, "It was a different time, wasn't it? Different standards."

Isabelle stood up and walked behind her grandmother's chair. She put her hands on her neck and started massaging her shoulders. Claire stiffened. Isabelle could feel the tension in every muscle. Claire cleared her throat loudly and fidgeted, and then slowly, as Isabelle's hands continued their soothing process, the tension began to ease in the old woman's shoulders until it had melted completely.

She turned and smiled shyly at her granddaughter. "Where did you learn how to do this?" She chuckled and added, "Maybe you could do my feet, sometime. I have such poor circulation in my lower body."

"Of course, Mamie, tomorrow. We'll ask Florence for a nice bowl of warm water and I'll get some salts in town."

Mamie settled back into her chair and closed her eyes. "Now, about the river— you're sure you did not see any vipers? It's so wild, down there. I am told that weeds have overtaken everything. Vipers love these wild places."

"They also love to dwell in people's imaginations. They call it the 'unconscious' mind."

"Unconscious? Where's that?"

"A hidden place within the mind, a place where a lot of fears come from. Actually, it is a wild place, just like the weeds at the river. Thoughts and emotions come straight out of it. I had a dream about a snake once that I want to tell you about. The snake was next to an ermine scarf in my dream. It looked dead, but it stood up fiercely when Mother reached for it. Is there an ermine scarf in our family, Mamie? "

Mamie straightened up abruptly. "Oh, that old thing. It's somewhere in the attic, probably all eaten up by moths by now."

"Isn't it strange that it came into my dream when I didn't know anything about it? That's the unconscious. Mother knew about it, too, and said that it belonged to her Aunt Justine. Can you tell me something about that scarf?"

"Absolutely not. My sister is dead, now, God rests her soul, and I will not tarnish her memory."

"Tarnish?"

"Isabelle, stop asking me questions like these. I don't want to talk about it. You can look for the thing, if you wish, but no more questions about Justine. Is it clear? I'm getting tired, now. Please take me back to the house. I want to watch television. I like to watch *La roue de la fortune* before dinner. It's one of these simple American game shows. We're invaded by American shows and movies, by American everything. Progress, they say. Ha, we sure don't need that." Claire mumbled on about the decadence of French life under the American influence while Isabelle pushed her grandmother back to the dining room where she settled happily to watch the American game show on the small TV screen.

Isabelle went to see Florence in the kitchen. She dipped a spoon into a soup Florence was stirring and sipped it. "Umm, delicious. Florence, did you know my Aunt Justine?"

"I only started working for Claire after she had her hip surgery and that was a long time after Justine had died."

"Are there any family papers, letters, or other documents around the house?"

"A few in an old desk in the dining room, along with some photographs. It's all pretty dusty."

"Clothes?"

"In the attic. A vintage clothing shop would love them but Mamie isn't ready to sort through the boxes and trunks yet."

"I'll risk it tomorrow. I suppose we have to wait until the end of the decadent *roue de la fortune* before we eat that soup, don't we?"

Florence grinned. "Mamie rules, Isabelle."

IN THE MORNING, Isabelle decided that she would start with the attic. She put on her comfy jeans and an old shirt of Pépé's she found hanging in her closet. Then she lugged a garden ladder upstairs and leaned it against the wall next to a trap door cut into the hall ceiling. The door was stuck all around from disuse so she had to pound all the edges with her fist until it gave way. Suddenly the whole thing tilted down, barely missing her head, and a cloud of dust came flying out of the attic. After Isabelle sneezed a few times and caught her balance on the ladder, she realized the door was hinged along one edge and she lifted it up and onto the attic floor and then climbed through the opening on her knees.

The room was quite dark and stuffy. There was only one skylight under the eaves and it was partially obscured by dust and debris. Isabelle stood up and walked carefully in, groping with her hands, and testing the floor with each footstep. The planks squeaked but seemed sturdy enough to hold her weight.

After her eyes became used to the semi-darkness, she began to distinguish the furniture and the objects scattered all around: a broken crib, painted what had once been a cream color, with horsehair bulging out of a torn mattress; a small chest, missing the bottom drawer, leaning on its left side against a taller wooden chest—as if looking for protection from a big brother; an antique metal bed frame, propped up against a wall; some kitchen utensils, irons, pots, and pans piled in a huge laundry basket; bunches of rags, heaped on the floor; an enormous *lessiveuse*, a wash basin with a massive cover, used in the old days to boil the white laundry items on an open fire. Isabelle stumbled over a couple of small metal boxes that had contained coffee or spices at one time, they were rusty, the inscriptions on them almost illegible. She finally saw two huge trunks in a corner of the attic. "Aha," she asked the dust and the beams, "the ermine stole?" One of the trunks was open and empty. She closed the top and its loud squeak filled the neglected room.

The other trunk was closed, with a key inside of the lock. Isabelle turned the key slowly, her heart beating very fast, as if she were entering a forbidden territory. A strong whiff of mothballs greeted her. They were scattered on a newspaper covering the contents of the trunk. Isabelle picked the papers up by the corners, cupped the mothballs in the center, and put them on the floor several feet away from her. Neatly folded garments and other treasures filled the big mystery trunk. She carefully took out, one by one, a beautiful collection of dresses and coats, out of the twenties and the thirties. She lifted each out and let it fall open in front of her. Their pastel colors were faded; wrinkles and creases lay where the dress had been folded for decades. Some of them were adorned with beads, pearls, or silk flowers. There was one dress, in particular, that made Isabelle whisper, "So so lovely." It was pearl grey, sleeveless, made of a chiffon material so light that it floated when she took it out. It had a low cut neckline and a circle of pearls around the low waistline, which separated the top of the dress from a pleated skirt. The dress was lined with a pink chiffon sheath. "Exquisite," Isabelle said and set it on the top of the empty trunk. She next found several colorful feather boas, silk nightgowns, long white gloves, a few lace collars that had yellowed with time, a beautiful white lace shawl, and three beaded evening purses. "Florence was right. This is a vintage clothing treasure."

Isabelle reached the bottom and saw a last item, a purse bulging curiously in the dark cavern of the trunk. She opened the brass clasp and pulled out a small ermine stole with its yellowish fur ending in tiny black tipped paws. Her breath caught in her chest. "Just like my dream. Unbelievable." She examined it carefully, noticing some cuts near the head part that could have been made with a knife or with scissors. She couldn't tell. They were not the work of an insect. Isabelle tenderly replaced the clothes in the trunk, including the pearly gray dress, covered them back up with the paper and mothballs, and then tucked the ermine scarf under her arm. Before leaving the attic, she thought something flickered in the dark corner farthest from the window. She looked around to make sure she had not missed a mirror, perhaps swinging in its frame like the one she had seen in her dream. But the corner was empty. That would have been too much. She chuckled and stroked a paw on the ermine stole.

Satisfied and stunned about how her dream had been made real, Isabelle crawled backwards out of the attic, let her feet find the ladder rungs, then closed the trap door and descended.

"So, are you happy now, sneaky girl?" said a voice from the bottom of the stairs.

Isabelle was startled and almost missed a step. "Oh, Mamie, I had no idea you were there."

"You were making such a commotion. What did you find? Did the moths do a lot of damage?"

"No, everything was in excellent shape in the trunk except the stole. They're so beautiful—and the pearl grey dress, what an elegant piece. Did all of the clothes belong to Aunt Justine, Mamie?"

"She was always dressed like a queen. I guess you missed the hatbox. It's behind the trunk. Be sure to look at it the next time you go up."

"Look. I found the stole but it has cuts or tears in it? See?"

"Well, so it does." Mamie looked away quickly. "May be the moths did it. Come. Florence got some salts in town while you were rummaging around. She's warming some water now so you can massage my feet."

VI

The Spider Web

A whole week went by as fast as a hummingbird. They had been lazy days, marvelous long summer days for Isabelle who let herself be pampered by Florence who was now a friend. The two women talked a lot about Claire, of course, but also about the village, the old timers, some of whom Isabelle remembered vaguely, the need to get a new car to replace Claire's dated Citroen that had only two working gears, the changes in the landscape, like roads being paved and shrubs and trees being cut everywhere to make room for new houses. They commiserated about the high rate of unemployment in France. Florence was thankful for her job and hoping that Claire would live for many more healthy years, both because she had grown quite fond of the irascible old woman and because it was satisfying work. Some neighbors came to visit, curious to meet the American, and a couple of Claire's regular friends showed up to play a hand or two of cards, enjoying the tea and *petites madeleines* Florence baked for the occasion.

Isabelle felt more relaxed than she had in years. Florence's cooking was consistently topnotch, and the sun shone with Mediterranean brilliance every day. In spite of Claire's warnings about snakes, Isabelle walked every day, sometimes finding unchanged landscapes, like an old cemetery and the red cast of sunsets on distant mountains, and sometimes being appalled at the ugliness of twentieth-century roads and gas stations. She reflected on this contrast in her journal, wrote letters home to Marguerite, read Colette in French, and even took a couple naps. She also gave Claire foot massages before she went to bed every night. At first, she tried to coax family stories out of her grandmother but Claire was dismissive and curt so Isabelle gave up. She realized what Mamie needed most was to simply lean her head back and doze luxuriously as Isabelle massaged pink life back into her pale neglected toes.

One evening after dinner, Mamie looked across the table at Isabelle with a mysterious smile and pulled a small black box out of her skirt pocket.

"Here Isabelle, this is for you. I didn't wear gorgeous clothes like your Aunt Justine did, but I had some very lovely things. Pépé gave me this. I want you to have it."

Isabelle opened the small velvet jewelry box to find a ring with a rose-cut diamond mounted in the middle of two curving gold leaves. "Mamie, it's just beautiful," Isabelle exclaimed. She turned the ring over and over, admiring the intricate details, and slipped it on and off her right ring finger. "Look at the small lines of the leaves and how gently the stone sits in them like it's nesting." She leaned over and kissed Mamie's soft wrinkled cheek and smelled the scent of her lavender soap. "I don't know what to say. Thank you, thank you so much."

"This way, you'll never forget me." Claire dabbed at her eyes with the lace handkerchief she kept on her lap.

"Forget you? It would be impossible to forget you. You are a glorious force of nature, Grandmother." Isabelle looked at the ring with great pride. "It feels so wonderful to share something from Pépé with you."

"I wish he were here to see it on your hand." Claire abruptly sat up straight and sniffed. "If you wear it in the garden, though, I'll snatch it back faster than you can blink. Pépé ruined more good shirts with his infernal dirt and kept me busy with laundry night and day."

Isabelle wore it every night for dinner from then on, but she kept it on the bedside table during the day. No need to rile her grandmother if she happened to pluck a flower from Pépé's old garden.

ISABELLE GOT A LETTER from Marguerite. The summer tourist season was in full force, her mother wrote, and she had to make forays out to the local garage sales in nearby towns to keep her shelves stocked with antiques. Isabelle chuckled knowing that was exactly what Marguerite loved to do and also that the shelves in her shop would always be overflowing no matter how many tourists scavenged for treasures. That was its charm. She read on. "I am very familiar with Mamie's reluctance to talk about her sister and the past," Marguerite wrote in response to Isabelle's complaint that she couldn't pry anything out of Claire. "Don't get discouraged, though. She'll open up in her own good time. Go find Dr. Victor Brusseau. He can probably clear up some of the questions Claire refuses to answer."

Isabelle was curious to find this character who "has an answer for everything" as Marguerite put it. She found Florence reading in the kitchen while Claire was taking her nap. "Can you tell me where I can find this old Dr. Victor… ah, Brazeau, I think. My mother told me he knew the family well."

"You mean Brusseau, the crazy old fellow who lives in the wooded area, by the mill?"

Isabelle's Dream

"There is no house by the mill, Florence, I went there the other day. Everything is abandoned, the woods are gone, and there is a freeway running by…"

"No, not that mill, Isabelle, the one on the other side of the village, not far from the castle."

"Just at the entrance of the West Woods?"

"Yes. You can't miss it. It's a small stone house with a rose bush climbing on the wall. There is a pond on the side, a small fenced in vegetable garden and ducks walking all over the yard. Oh, yes, I almost forgot. There's an old wishing well in front of the house with pots of geraniums sitting on the edge." She laughed and shook her head. "I'll let you discover the rest—the crazy part."

"What do you mean?"

Florence leaned over and whispered with mock fear, "Clémentine, the wife, is some sort of a witch, people say."

"Nonsense," scoffed Isabelle.

"You're right. Actually, he used to be an excellent doctor, an unconventional one to say the least, but he made people well and that's what counts, right?"

"You've piqued my interest, that's for sure. Should I call them before I go?"

"No need. They don't have a telephone. Just go!"

Isabelle left while Claire was still asleep, knowing Mamie would scowl and discourage her from talking to anyone about her "private family matters. "I'm being a naughty little girl!" Isabelle whispered to herself as she closed the door quietly and walked quickly away from the house.

After a couple of miles, she reached the stone house by the woods. The place was exactly as Florence had described it, except that she had omitted to mention a little cemetery located by the garden. Four tiny little graves, made of raised earth, were outlined with seashells of different shapes and color. The graves were inscribed with white pebbles forming the names *Fido*, *Médor*, *Minouche*, and *Jacquot*. There were bright artificial flowers and more shells to finish the decorations on top of each grave. "It's a pet cemetery," Isabelle realized. "Catharine would love this place."

"You like my art work, Madame?"

Isabelle jumped and turned to see a tall, slender old man keenly observing her from the doorway of the stone house.

"Yes. I have a friend I'd love to show it to because she loves cemeteries and this one is really different!"

"Cemeteries have to be cheerful, don't you think?"

"It's a good idea under the circumstances." Isabelle stepped toward him with a smile. "My name is Isabelle. I'm Claire's granddaughter. You know Claire?"

"Who doesn't know Claire? So, you are the American, the schoolteacher who lives near San Francisco. I once met you briefly when you were four years old, just before you left for the States with Marguerite."

Isabelle was surprised to hear that Victor knew so much about her already, and she was about to ask, but he anticipated her question. "This is a small village and your grandmother is not particularly secretive, as you probably know."

"Actually, she's not too forthcoming about the past with me. That's why I'm here, I confess."

He looked at her with blue eyes under thick white eyebrows. His eyelids drooped halfway over his eyes but the effect was one of kindness and thoughtfulness. "Come in and meet my wife, Clémentine. You've arrived just in time. She's baking a cherry pie."

Isabelle followed Victor into the house. A heavenly sweet fragrance wafted out the door reminding Isabelle of the scents of her mother's place while she was cooking, inviting and alluring as she followed Victor into the kitchen.

He went and stood by his wife who was wiping flour off a counter. The two were a study in contrasts. Whereas Victor was tall and slender, Clémentine was short and plump in an apron that was covered in splotches of red cherry juice. Both were probably in their middle eighties. Victor was almost bald, had a large nose and deep circles under his intense blue eyes. His wife had a mop of tightly curled grey hair encircling her round face. Her squinting brown eyes fixed on Isabelle as she walked across the kitchen. Clémentine did not say a word; she stood close to her and just stared, which made Isabelle very uncomfortable. Victor handed Clémentine her glasses, at which point the eyes relaxed along with the whole body.

"I don't know you. Are you from around here?"

"It's Claire's granddaughter, the American. You remember Marguerite?"

"Oh yes. A lovely child. Married an American after the war."

"This is her daughter Isabelle."

"Ah, now I know who you are. It's so nice of you to visit. If you can wait a little while, we'll have some cherry pie and tea and you can tell us all about your country. Victor, take Isabelle in the dining room. I'll join you as soon as this thing is ready."

Victor led Isabelle into a large sunny room that served as a dining and living area. There were houseplants scattered all around and they gave the place a warm tropical look. Isabelle sat down on one of the white wicker armchairs surrounding a small table and looked around. Whimsical figurines decorated every shelf in the room. There were frogs, dwarfs, elves, spiders, a Hansel and Gretel ginger bread house, a little mermaid, Pinocchio, Cinderella trying on a slipper, Blue Beard holding his wife by the hair, and a large framed Walt Disney Snow White poster above the piano.

"My wife collected these figurines for our grandchildren to enchant them when they visited. Of course, they're all grown up now, but she can't bring herself to get rid of their toys. Clémentine loves fairy tales."

"I think it's important to keep a child's wonder when you are… in your eighties, I suspect?"

Victor nodded. "We are both eighty-five—going on five, as you can see."

"I understand you've known my mother's side of the family for many years."

Victor sat down across from her and nodded. "Sixty years, maybe. I was the only doctor in the village for a long time, and I knew everybody, of course. In the 1960s, the village started growing and two more physicians moved in. I retired in the '70s." He paused and sat back. "Yes, I've known your relatives quite well. They all used to spend their summers here, and then your grandparents retired to the summer home permanently, just a few years before I retired."

"Then you knew my grand aunt Justine, too?"

"Oh yes. A lovely woman. Quite stylish."

"She had the most beautiful clothes. I recall a lovely white lace shawl that complemented all her dresses.

"I found that in the attic but I don't remember her. I was only two when she died."

"The prettiest woman I've ever seen—except Clémentine, of course. She had dark brown hair, a peachy complexion, beautiful brown eyes." He paused and looked up as if to see her in his mind's eye. "Her eyes looked especially kind. She made some amazing hats, very creative."

"Was there anything—what would be the word—*shameful* about her life? Mamie said something puzzling about not wanting to tarnish her memory."

"Your grandmother is probably referring to the fact that Justine lived 'in sin' with a wealthy man without ever getting married. In those days, this type of situation was scandalous. But I also think—in fact, I know—that Claire was very jealous of her sister. She will probably tell you more about it."

"She refuses to talk about Justine. Believe me, I've tried."

Victor laughed, and it surprised Isabelle that it was as deep and strong as a younger man's laugh. "Wait until she gets into a fit of anger, then she'll spill the beans."

"I am very interested in my family background, Victor. Actually, I am trying to explain a very powerful dream I had earlier in the year. The characters in the dream were all women on my mother's side of the family. There was a snake, too…"

"The snake is Claire's phobia, her nemesis. Claire has never wanted to take a look at the spider webs in her own basement!"

"The spider webs?"

"What do I hear about spider webs? Victor, you're not in your office, anymore, and Isabelle isn't your patient. You're going to get her all confused." Clémentine interjected as she walked into the room with a large tray. "Let's have a nice tea party with our guest, and maybe she can tell us what's so great about the States that our grandson has renounced his own country to live there!"

"So, your grandson lives in America? Where?"

"In New York. Philippe is an artist, he paints weird abstract huge… I don't know what. He says that New York is the place where he gets inspired. I don't understand his paintings at all. He is coming to visit next week, so you'll probably get to meet him," Clémentine added, setting a cup in front of Isabelle into which she poured some steaming tea.

"Would you like a slice of lemon? I've cut the pie already and made small portions. You can have another piece if this is not enough for you, Isabelle. We eat very little ourselves."

"No, this is just right, thank you. And I'll take a lemon slice."

Isabelle took a forkful of pie. It was still warm and not too sweet. Clémentine let the fresh cherries speak for themselves. The piecrust melted in her mouth, just like the crust that Marguerite always made. It's the butter, she thought and smiled because that's what her mother said whenever she complimented her crust.

Clémentine looked at her curiously.

"Your crust is exquisite. It's the butter, my mother always used to say."

"French butter," Clémentine added.

Next Isabelle brought the tea to her lips. She let the scent fill her nose. It was an exotic blend of hibiscus flowers, orange peel, cinnamon, and rose hips with a hint of licorice. A delightful mixture! These people are wonderful, Isabelle thought, and I can't see where the craziness begins, unless perhaps in the basement with those spider webs?

"Victor, can you tell me more about these spider webs which my grandmother has not looked at. They sound intriguing."

"It's a long story, Isabelle. I used this image with my patients when I wanted them to look at their lives, if I felt that their problems were more than just physical. As it is for most of our ills, as you probably know. Sometimes their ailments were directly related to a family trait, something in the genes or the influences they had grown up with. Most of the time they weren't aware of it, and I told them to look for answers in that network of spider webs which dwelled in their basement."

"Modern psychology couldn't have put it better, Victor. Another one is the mess of wild weeds where Claire's fear of vipers resides."

Clémentine put her cup down and poured each of them more tea. "And I think the image of the basement with the spider webs is so mysterious and romantic. You can imagine groping your way through it, being afraid of disturbing the webs, falling into holes and tunnels, clearing a path. Victor's patients thought that he was a little odd to speak in those terms. It was long before psychology became a household word. But some of them got the message and they did find answers in their basements, cleared some of their spider webs, and got well," Clémentine added, excitingly.

"I have always believed," Victor continued, "that there was more to a patient than his or her ailing body. I am convinced that our ancestors speak to us, and that we inherit certain personalities from them, as well as fears, anger, and humor. The negative aspects can even make us sick. When we recognize this, we can see what age-old conflicts harm us and then begin to heal." He looked at Clémentine and his lips broke into an impish grin. "Of course, some people refuse to believe in this. Nonsense, they call it. Those ones get pills."

"Victor, this is exactly what I've been studying for a year or two. And it's just what I came for this summer: to look into my family background after I had this puzzling dream. Where do I begin to walk throught the spider webs?"

"I always told my patients to look at family papers, photos, letters, ask questions like the ones you've started asking Marguerite and Claire. Think of your own problems and qualities and see whom you relate to. Sometimes traits jump a generation."

Clémentine leaned forward and said, "Now one other thing: if there are women in your mother's background whose birth date has nine months difference with yours, one way or the other, then you'll feel a stronger connection."

Isabelle looked skeptical. "But… "

Clémentine dropped her chin and looked at Isabelle sternly. The old woman's glasses slipped down to the middle of her nose and her eyes peered over the top of the frames. "Mark my words, young lady! Victor is right about webs of ancestors but don't forget there is always an element of magic in these matters."

"It's true. Clémentine's theory about birth dates has been proved to me again and again in my long time observation of my patients. Don't discount any possibilities that connect you to beings from the past," Victor concluded in a serious tone.

"Since I was born in March, this would mean… " Isabelle tried to do the math in her head.

"December or June—or close to it."

"You'll have fun doing this, Isabelle," Clémentine added with a grin. She pushed her glasses back up her nose and left a white flour fingerprint on the lens. "After you get the information, come back to see us, and I'll show you why your life is like a fairy tale!"

Isabelle took leave of her new friends, puzzled and intrigued, but lighthearted, too. She passed the shell-decorated pet cemetery and recalled the whimsical fairy tale characters in the dining room. Her effort to unearth the past was serious but she liked the sense of play Victor and Clémentine Brusseau had offered. She imagined spider webs in her basement and a line of ancestors she could dance with, one after the other. *There you go, Isabelle* lightly scolded herself as she headed up the road to the park, once again the hopeless romantic. *Dancing with ancestors under spider webs.* Yet, she had such a good feeling about these people that she decided to trust her guts and to really look into what they had suggested. "Anyway, what do I have to lose?" she said to the setting sun.

Florence was putting soup and a baguette on the table as Isabelle walked into the dining room. Claire turned her head around and scowled. "I suppose you've been looking for snakes again."

"Not at all. I went to visit Dr. Victor Brusseau and his wife, Clémentine. She made the most delicious cherry pie and I hardly have room for dinner."

Claire noisily sipped her soup and yanked a hunk of bread from the baguette. "The old nut probably told you all his foolishness about spider webs. And Clémentine, so childlike with her toys. Not all there if you ask me." And Claire tapped her head with a finger.

"I think that's a little mean, Mamie. She was lovely. And frankly, with all due respect, I went there to find out about our family. Whatever your reasons, Mamie, you don't want to help me beyond sending me up to the attic. I had to look elsewhere."

The room was suddenly very quiet and still. Mamie looked down at her half-empty bowl and fingered the breadcrumbs on the table. Isabelle felt bad for being so harsh. She reached over and touched her grandmother's hand. "I'm sorry. You have your reasons and I respect them. Anyway, Victor simply told me to dig through family papers and other mementos, this doesn't sound too insane, does it? I would even say that it sounds more like granting a respectful consideration to these people I am related to, wouldn't you agree?"

Mamie still sat very still but answered, "I am not so sure."

"You are an amazing woman. Someday a great great great great granddaughter of yours might be so interested in your life. Wouldn't you want her to know you and what you meant to all of us in this family and community?"

"I suppose. Go ahead, Isabelle, look wherever you choose. The house is full of mementos, but you'll be disappointed, because there is nothing to learn. We just weren't that interesting." Mamie suddenly looked very tired.

Isabelle squeezed her hand and smiled. "My dreams have told me otherwise."

ISABELLE WOKE UP EARLY because a hard rain was pelting the metal shutters, and the room was chilly. She crawled further down into her bed, bringing the covers over her head. A perfect rainy day to rummage through family papers, she thought, stretching her whole body. What had she learned about it so far? Claire was threatened by her exploration into family matters. Perhaps because there had been a serious rivalry between her and Justine. Marguerite was a definite link because she was the one who had made the snake come alive in her dream. The ermine scarf was an emissary from the world of the past to the present. But how this all might evolve her own life was still a puzzle. Nothing quite fit together yet. As she relaxed under the down comforter and let the rain lull her, Isabelle even wondered whether she still had any problems. She closed her eyes. Problems? Don't forget about men. Nothing resolved about that at all—simply postponed.

It was Claire's day for her bi-monthly trip to the hairdresser with Florence. Though it was raining very hard, the old woman insisted, "That little rain won't stop me." She added with a stern expression, "The train has to run on time and I will keep it running, no matter what. I am not like those communist strikers."

Florence winked at Isabelle while shrugging her shoulders stoically. She went outside to the garage and brought the car as close as she could to the front door. Isabelle grabbed the umbrella—large enough to cover three people— and pushed Mamie to the open car door. She lifted her by the shoulders and slid her into the front seat. Then she folded the wheelchair and slid it into the back seat. "Don't worry, Florence, I'll close the gate." She followed the car down the driveway and closed the gate behind it.

First Isabelle made a second cup of coffee and headed for the sitting room, happy to have the house all to herself. She sat at the old desk and sipped her café au lait. "Where do I start?" She sighed and pulled out piles of birth certificates, death certificates, marriage certificates, baptismal records, sepia colored photos, property deeds, war food stamps, train tickets, small diaries, hotel bills, postcards and ledgers from the old desk drawers. The stacks looked impenetrable and Isabelle felt discouraged. The miscellaneous details of two or three generations and probably several secret lives were hiding behind the cryptic papers. Isabelle thumbed through one of the diaries which contained information on household expenses, weather patterns, some events of World War One, and remarkable happenings in the family, like the date of a wedding or of a funeral. Another diary was somewhat similar, important dates, large purchases, the day a hen started to sit on some eggs—which made Isabelle chuckle out loud—and a trip to Paris by train with a daily account of the visit to the 1937 international fair. There was much history but not a single expression of personal feelings in either diary, nothing human, nothing which betrayed a passing emotion, just facts, recorded minutely. It was so different from her own diaries that were full of every tumultuous emotion that rose and fell during her day. "Did these people only live by the clock?" whispered Isabelle, disappointed. She looked at some of the post cards, some of them very old, whose stamps had been removed. The short messages were almost all the same: *Beautiful place, Having a wonderful time, Wish you could be here with us, See you soon.*

Let down by her so far fruitless search, Isabelle went to the kitchen and stole one of Florence's *madeleines*. She took her cookie back to the old desk again, knowing she needed a new strategy. Perhaps she should follow Clémentine's advice and start looking at birth certificates for that weird nine-month before and after her birth date connection. She popped the rest of the treat into her mouth and started opening the official transcripts.

Recorded in elegant cursive writing by city hall officers a long time ago, the French certificates were a detailed account of recorded events, especially those processed before 1850. They included information on the nuptial protagonists as well as on the witnesses—on their line of work, where they lived, whether the children were legitimate and so on. Isabelle marveled at the two page-account of her great great great grandmother's wedding, in 1849. It was a lyrical narrative of the groom's background: He was the legitimate son of a coal miner, who with his mother's consent, took a very young wife named Babette. The girl's mother was a factory worker, present at the signing and willing to agree to the wedding. The event had been planned by the two parties and officially published for the last month and *to which no opposition had been made*. Next came the detailed list of the witnesses and, finally, an account of the ceremony and the signing. Nothing was said about a religious marriage ceremony.

Isabelle read and read and read. She began to organize the data on a wide table into a sort of a family tree, with all the dates of birth and death of all these people and their professions. There were some coal miners and gunsmiths among the men, mostly textile workers and dressmakers among the women. After 1900, the certificates were less detailed and did not mention professions any more.

With the rain creating a soothing patter in the background, Isabelle looked at the tree laid out before her. What did these names, dates, and professions say to her about these people's lives? They had hard lives. Isabelle then looked for the birth dates. Which women among them had been born in June or in December? She located four names: the great great great grandmother Babette, whose lengthy wedding certificate she had read; Babette's daughter who was her great great grandmother: her grand aunt Justine; and, of course, her own mother who was born in June. So there is something about each of these lives I must pay attention to, Isabelle thought. The only interesting pattern she could see was that three of these women had lost their husbands when they were very young: two men had died in coal mining accidents and her own father, of course, died fighting in the resistance. Justine had not married. Isabelle didn't know how to take the connection any further and decided that she would eventually talk to Victor for further help.

She picked up a stack of photos of serious looking people in old fashioned garbs, chubby naked babies lying on white rugs, brides with crowns made of orange flower blossoms and children on long swings hanging from trees. The wartime ration books reminded her how hard it had been for them to get food during the last war. Each stamp coupon was marked with a different letter J1, J3, A. What did that mean?

As Isabelle returned the documents to their proper drawers and slots, returning the past to its dormant home in the desk. The rain almost sounded like a ghostly voice of the silent mementos saying, "We are part of you, Isabelle We are your breath, blood, and heart."

The rain stopped suddenly and the light quickly changed, brightening in a disorienting way. Isabelle looked at the clock: "One thirty already! What could those two be doing all this time?" and at that moment, she heard the wooden lock being lifted off the gate.

Claire was flushed and excited when she entered the house. "I took Florence to lunch after my appointment. We went to the new Italian restaurant. It actually wasn't bad."

"Claire ate two bowls of pasta and a plate of bread."

"Aren't you starving, Isabelle?"

"I didn't realize it was so late. I'll go fix myself a sandwich… "

Mamie waved her hands dismissively. "That's not a proper lunch, Isabelle, that's an American lunch! Florence will warm up some leftovers for you, and we bought some good goat cheese at the farm on the way back."

Isabelle sat in the dining room and had a warm lunch while her grandmother drank her mint tisane.

"Did you find anything interesting in all those papers, Isabelle?"

"A few things, Mamie. Apparently our ancestors were all working people."

"Yes, the St. Etienne area, where most of them were from, was a coal mining, weapon manufacturing, and textile processing region. A 19th-century industrial center. My own father worked in a foundry and my mother in a weaving mill. They were very good people, respectable, hard working, actually quite poor. I grew up learning how to make my own clothes. Times were very difficult, especially during World War One. A terrible influenza killed a lot of people, but of course, things started changing after I married your Pépé. He came from a wealthy family and my life got a lot easier. But I always kept a strong respect for hard work and frugal living."

"Did Aunt Justine marry a wealthy man, also?" Isabelle asked timidly.

"You didn't find her wedding certificate, did you?"

"No."

"There's your answer. I already told you that I don't want to talk about her."

"Don't be so grumpy, Claire," said Florence. "She's naturally curious."

"Oh, I suppose. Isabelle, did you see the photographs? I'll tell you who is who if you're interested."

"I'd love that, and what about all the war coupons? What do J2, J3, and A mean?"

"Because of food restrictions The Vichy had different categories of allowances according to your age: E for *enfant*, got more milk, then the Js stood for the young people, with a little more food as they grew. J3 were the teenagers who got the most. A, the adults, came next, and finally the V, the old people, got less food than the A category. Some old people nearly starved to death, especially in big cities."

"That sounds so cruel."

"It was the same for my parents, too," added Florence. "People were so thin. You can see it in photos. There was a food-coupon black market, of course, but you had to be careful."

"I know, Mother told me about it. She also said that you were the mainstay of the family, Mamie. Always coming up with extra. Out of nothing."

"My survival skills, Isabelle. They came in handy."

Claire and Isabelle sat close together, going through the photos. Claire described which generation they were, where they lived, who had survived the wars and who hadn't. There wasn't a single picture of Justine, but Isabelle didn't mention it. The timing wasn't right.

VII

The Ermine Scarf

The next day, Isabelle jotted down some of the information gathered from the various certificates and bought a blooming houseplant as she walked through town on the way to Victor and Clémentine's cottage. As she walked up to the front door of their cottage, she smelled the sweet scents of chocolate and butter. Clémentine was baking again. Isabelle knocked, and hearing Clémentine's greeting, walked down the hall to the kitchen. Clémentine pushed a tray full of little mounds of chocolate dough deep into the oven, stood up, and wiped her hands on a towel. She turned to Isabelle with a grin and said, "Philippe is coming next week, and I want to be ready. Oh look. You've brought some azaleas. Thank you, Isabelle, I love them."

Isabelle placed them in the middle of the table. "Philippe is your son?"

"My grandson. And he loves chocolate drop cookies. I am sure he doesn't eat good French food in New York. That must be an awful town with all the crime, overcrowding, pollution." She clucked her tongue in disapproval.

"Yes," Isabelle nodded, "but when it comes to the arts, there is no place in the world like New York." Clémentine looked at her askance. "Except for Paris, of course." Isabelle added with a smile.

Victor walked in with a basket of freshly cut vegetables. He dropped a handful of cherry tomatoes in her palm and set his basket on the table.

She popped the ripe fruit in her mouth. "These are sweet as candy. Look at that lettuce, and I've never seen such a color purple of those eggplants."

"Too much work, though, I am getting a little old for this kind of exercise." He stretched his back. "Bending down kills my back, but as Voltaire said in *Candide*, in order to find happiness, *Il faut cultiver votre jardin*."

"Shall we have tea, again? You can sample some of my cookies; the first batch'll be ready in ten minutes"

Isabelle sat in the white wicker armchair and told Victor about her trip into the past. She showed him the family tree diagram she had composed from the certificates in the old desk. Victor looked at it carefully, examining the dates, the places mentioned, concentrating on the four women whose birth dates had a special nine months link to Isabelle's. He remained silent for a long time.

"Isabelle, you've received a very strong message from three of your women relatives. Each had a man abandon her, then leave her alone to fend for herself, to raise the children, to work hard. This was the life of these great grandmothers and your own mother after their young husbands died." He raised his eyebrow at her. "Yes?"

"That's the story of my life, too. I've never been able to keep a man, no matter what I did, no matter how hard I tried." Her voice caught in her throat.

Victor reached across the family tree and touched her hand. "The spider web is intricately woven around you."

"But that makes me powerless, doesn't it? At the whim of the past?"

"Being able to see how entwined you are with the past is the first step toward becoming liberated from it." He smiled and nodded vigorously. "It will happen."

Clémentine arranged plates and cups on the small table while listening to the last part of the conversation. She gazed compassionately at Isabelle and put her hands gently on the younger woman's shoulders.

"Remember what I told you about things in your life happening like in a fairy tale? Close your eyes for a minute, Isabelle. Imagine."

Isabelle swallowed the sob that had been rising in her throat, sighed, and closed her eyes.

"Two magical beings hovered over your mother when you were in the womb, each pollinating you with truths from your ancestry. One being represented the shadow—what you just found out about the dark burden carried by the women in your family sounds very much like a shadow on your life, or in simpler terms, a curse. Yes?" Isabelle nodded slowly. "But don't forget the other little rascal. She rained light and depth of thought and character into you, too. These are the things you discover and re-discover in bits and pieces until, at some time in your life, you're completely receptive to hearing her more complicated voice. Perhaps that is coming now. A light, a bigger romance than the ones that have evaded you with men. It is the romance with all of life, with yourself." Clémentine threw up her hands with a wild little giggle. Isabelle snapped open her eyes.

Victor gave a clap with his rough gardener's hands. "You're a romantic, Isabelle. How grand. But look," he tapped the family tree, "don't forget this woman, Aunt Justine. The spider drew a strong thread between you. There are some discoveries to be made here."

"Claire doesn't want to talk about her."

"Give her some time. She has the same shadows in her life that you do—without as much faith in the gifts of life. Her life was hard."

Isabelle was overwhelmed. The shadow over her relationships with men seemed insurmountable. She felt irritated that Claire was a stumbling block to her change but Victor was telling her to be compassionate. She suddenly wanted to be alone. Isabelle finished her tea and cookies quickly. She stood and hugged Victor first, and then Clémentine. Clémentine held her cheeks and said, "Thank you for the azaleas, dear. Did you know they are very meaningful?"

Isabelle looked at her with curiosity.

"Yes, they are a symbol of caring for yourself, of fragile passion. The Chinese consider them a symbol of womanhood. Now off with you. Come back to meet Philippe on Sunday afternoon."

"I'm sorry. I'm a little disoriented by our talk."

Victor took her arm and led her to door. "Not to worry. It's to be expected." He frowned at the sky. "Hurry home."

Dark clouds were forming in the sky as well as Isabelle's mind. "The shadow and the light. Jungian nonsense." Isabelle mumbled as she walked back to her grandmother's house. Disquieted, she could feel her heart racing and her neck break into a sweat. She opened up her blouse, trying to cool herself. "These people are so witchy and silly. I'm fifty years old and I've been in the most sophisticated therapies for years. I'm like a stupid mouse in a stupid maze. Shadow. Light. Shadow. Light. Give me a break. I'm just a fool about men and in an endless, endless pattern over it." She grumbled out loud, "Get over it, woman."

The clouds got darker and darker, clumping together, rolling, and threatening. Isabelle saw a lightning zigzag over the mountain but raced in the front door just as sheets of rain swept across the park. Isabelle walked directly into the dining room where Claire was finishing her afternoon snack. The old lady raised her head up, suspicion written all over her puckered lips.

"So, you went back to consult with the village witches. What did they have to reveal to you this time?" Claire snickered.

Isabelle felt rage rise into her throat. She felt she would burst if she didn't speak her mind but the words were blocked deep inside, knotted, tangled up. She looked at Claire sitting on her throne, toying with her. And she wanted to run a sword through the thick armor. She wanted to shatter this old woman's arrogance. She remained quiet, for a moment, then, following a strong impulse overcoming her fear. "Here we go," she said to herself, breathing deeply, as she looked at her stern grandmother, straight in the eyes.

"Yes Mamie, I saw Victor and his wife today, and we talked about Aunt Justine. She was the prettiest woman, artistic, kind and talented, wasn't she?"

Claire's face became livid, she gasped intensely for a couple seconds, her mouth tightening as if she were in pain, and then as if Isabelle had poked an enormous abscess, the wound opened.

"Justine was no good. Everybody looked at her pretty face and thought she was better than anybody else. I hated her. When we were kids, she was always the favorite. Justine here, Justine there. There was never anything for me, always her, and she laughed and she joked and she flirted. She thought she was so cute, but she was a disgrace and she proved it. When she started shacking up with that boyfriend of hers—a nobleman if you please—the family was dishonored. They never got married, but *Madame* continued to flaunt her lifestyle, her pretty clothes, and her jewelry. I was working as a secretary. She would come and pick me up at the office sometimes, wearing a gorgeous coat and that ermine scarf, and I would be so ashamed. She looked like a prostitute. I was so ashamed. The woman never worked hard in her life, she never had any kids, she never knew what it is to struggle. And I struggled all my life—struggled, I'm telling you. Isabelle, you just don't know, you just don't know."

Claire was crying. She started crying softly at first, then deep sobs began to heave out of her chest, louder and louder, until they became so strong that Isabelle got scared. How could she help stop this flood of misery pouring from her grandmother? What have I done? she thought.

Isabelle walked to the back of Claire's chair and put her hands on the old lady's neck, and massaged the tight shoulders. "You must have suffered very much, Mamie. It must be hard to struggle all the time, feel that someone else thinks they're better than you are. I know. I often feel that I am never good enough, too. But that's not true. I am learning how good I am, deep down, and you are too. Oh Mamie please, I didn't want to hurt you."

Both women were crying now. Isabelle put her head next to her grandmother's face, encircling her shoulders with her arms. Their tears mixed like a warm soothing balm as they cried their need to love, their need to heal the long struggles handed down from generations past, the rivalry that had poisoned Claire's life, the abandonment that had cursed Isabelle's. They cried for the factory worker relatives of theirs and the widows, the seamstresses, and the single mothers. They were crying for

Justine, Germaine, and Marguerite, for all women left to hold the pieces of life together while men wandered.

Claire broke the silence first, sniffing her tears back. She looked towards the window. "Look Isabelle, the storm is over, it's stopped raining." She gave a great, deep sigh. "I think I'll sleep well tonight. I feel very tired."

"I'm tired, too. Let's go to bed right after dinner, Mamie, after I do your foot massage. I'll ask Florence to serve dinner early."

"Yes. And Isabelle, there's something else I didn't tell you." She looked down at her gnarled hands and wrung them slowly in a piece of her shawl. "I did cut up Justine's ermine stole one day. I was so angry," Claire looked up with her old defiance. "It felt good even though now I am ashamed, very ashamed of myself."

"I understand."

"Justine was a beautiful woman, and she really didn't look like a prostitute. She was also kind and generous. I was jealous because my parents, everybody else and even you Isabelle, paid so much attention to her."

"Parents do these things sometimes. They don't know how it hurts. I've seen it in the parents of my students. Children can't speak for themselves. They hide their pain and they deal with it the best way they can. I'm honored to be your granddaughter, you know. That's why I'm here. You're the most resilient woman I've ever met and I feel such respect for you."

"Resilient? I feel so tired."

Dinner was a quiet one. Florence seemed concerned that Claire looked so exhausted. Isabelle had explained to her, without going into so many details, that she and her grandmother had settled a painful family problem. But Florence couldn't understand why Claire's feistiness had suddenly evaporated. Florence told Isabelle after dinner that she would take Claire to the doctor the following day if she still looked depressed.

Isabelle gave Claire her evening foot massage, translating her loving feelings into gentle touch. Claire was silent. Isabelle longed for her to speak, to be the frisky old lady she was used to, but she had to settle for a quiet "Good night Isabelle, and thank you for the rub."

Isabelle went up to her room. It was only eight and still full daylight outside. She was exhausted, too, after such an emotional day, but also tense. "Where are my hot tub and my classical music when I need them?" She sighed. "I would give anything to sink into a warm womb and hear some Mozart, right now. Have a massage—or even make love." Isabelle decided to settle for a short meditation. She sat by the open window, closed her eyes, cleared her mind, and remained very still, breathing in the lovely evening air.

After twenty-five minutes of deep stillness, she opened her eyes, and felt better than she had in many, many months. Her mind immediately resumed its quest. Isabelle opened the armoire where she had put the ermine stole and brought it back to her chair. She stretched the fur piece on her lap, rubbing its hair softly. There it was, silent witness of the long held grudge and symbol of that bitter rivalry. She looked at the awkward cuts, imagining the anger that had prompted the slashing. She could almost feel a tremble in the fur as she recalled Claire's tirade. This emotion had poisoned Claire's life, making her feel inferior and unloved. It was so powerful that it had resonated into Marguerite's and her own life as well, finding its way into the mighty dream which had compelled Isabelle to begin her search. "The spider webs have hung tightly in the basement for years, now they are beginning to float away in the wind," she thought smiling.

It was now past nine and Isabelle started to wonder how her grandmother was doing. She had looked so emotionally drained. Was she lying in bed, crying, or perhaps feeling guilty or ashamed? Isabelle started to tiptoe down the steps. Halfway down, a loud snore came from Claire's room. "A resilient woman, she is," whispered Isabelle, laughing and nodding her head as she climbed back up to her room. "A resilient old woman."

As she sank down into her bed, Isabelle decided that her mission was almost completed. She now had the pieces of the puzzle and her dream was clear. She had looked into the mirror at herself and at her unconscious and she had remembered to smile while doing it. She had seen the group of women dressed in black who had vanished in the sunny mist and identified them. They were the carriers of the message about men, they were the widows, the ones Isabelle knew as well as she now knew herself. Her mother had triggered the confrontation with the buried jealous rivalry between Justine and Claire by encouraging her daughter to take the trip in her place and by kicking the snake, the cottonmouth, hissing as Claire had done earlier. The discovery of the furry scarf, the ermine stole, had allowed the revelation to occur. Isabelle could hear the voice of her therapist, Professor Handley saying, "The way is now paved for a transformation." The snake was no longer a threat.

She put the ermine aside, closed the window, and got ready for bed. As she slipped under the covers, she realized she had one more thing to do now that the shadow was returned to the past. She needed to find the light that was Justine's life and apply it to her own. "But that's probably the easy

Isabelle's Dream

part," she muttered, stretching until she could reach her toes far into the bed with the greatest feeling of relief. Isabelle went to sleep with a sense of gratitude and happiness.

Claire was up and rummaging in the desktop drawer when Isabelle came down the next morning. She seemed well and totally oblivious of what had happened the previous day.

"Good morning Mamie. You're up and around early. Did you sleep well?"

"Not a wink." Isabelle grinned remembering the lion's snore that came from Mamie's room. Her grandmother handed her a little key. "Be careful when you open the old secretary in your room, Isabelle. The key doesn't fit very well and you have to wiggle it to the right. There are some of Justine's old letters I believe. I've never read them myself because, well… Justine is gone now, but you go ahead."

Isabelle took the key and turned it gently over in her hands, sensing it would release the light held captive in her family history. She hoped that somehow the women from her past would feel it in a mysterious way, too.

"By the way, Florence said that she wanted to take me to see the doctor. Tell her it's not necessary. I'm not sick."

"I will, Mamie. I'm going to the village, this morning. I'll stop at the pharmacy if you wish."

"I told you, Isabelle, I'm not sick. An old lady like me doesn't need much anymore, just some foot massages from her granddaughter. Let's eat. I'll die right now if I don't get my café au lait."

After breakfast, Isabelle got stamps at the post office. She also went to the market and bought two bouquets of flowers and a bottle of champagne to celebrate all their revelations. When she came home, she handed the bouquet to Claire and another to Florence who accepted hers with an effusion of thanks.

"What's the occasion, Isabelle?" Claire, asked, "It's not my name day nor my birthday nor Florence's either."

"We're going to celebrate, Mamie, just the three of us. We'll drink champagne at lunch, today!"

"Like three wicked little old ladies," Claire added with a grin.

"Yes Mamie, just like that. Three very wicked women. And we'll toast to the most resilient and dynamic of all: you."

Florence raised her hand. "I'll vouch for that."

The lunch of baguette, cheese, hard sausage, and sliced tomatoes was good in that simple but elegant French manner. The champagne was cold and dry. Claire became very tipsy after her second glass and sang, "*Le temps des cerises.*" Florence broke into the second verse with her. Isabelle laughed.

In the afternoon, when Mamie was once again snoring from her bedroom and even Florence claimed the need to nap, Isabelle went to her room and put the key into the secretary lock. She did not forget to wiggle it to the right, as Claire had suggested, and it worked. She rolled the top back. Surrounding a large white blotting pad, covered with blue ink imprints, were two stacks of letters, an ink well, several pens, two white porcelain candle holders, and a few small books piled on top of each other. One of the stacks of letters was held together with a pale pink ribbon, the other laced with a piece of twine. Isabelle felt at the same time a great curiosity and a strong sense of respect for these mementos, hesitating to move them out of their resting place. It was as if she was about to unearth Justine's ghost. It had been different looking at her aunt's clothes. Now she was about to hear her voice in writing, enter her soul. She picked up the stack of letters held together with the twine first, untying the loops slowly, and she began to read them. The one on top of the stack had been written by Justine's lover's sister.

> *Dear Justine,*
>
> *I am returning these letters written by you to my dear brother, Edmond. I recently discovered them in his country home in Veyrier du lac after his death. I only read a few and they filled me with great sadness because, though we have never met, he once confided in me about the secret love he carried for many years in his heart for you. My dear Justine, I am sorry you two were never able to marry and fulfill the rich promise of your affections. It was an unfortunate situation with respect to Valérie. I cry too, every day over Edmond's untimely death because of his allegiance to France. We both know the terrible price our families and friends and nation have paid during this unspeakable time. I hope you, as I do, find strength in your faith. I have heard you are not well and wish you a prompt recovery from your illness.*

THE REST OF THE LETTERS were the love letters from Justine to Edmond. Isabelle settled on the chair by the window and began to journey into her grand aunt's world.

Poetic, romantic, touching, spiritual, sounding like a child one time, like a wise old woman another, Justine repeated her constant love to this man and her hope to be able to live with him as his wife, some day. She described her happiness at trips they had taken together, thanked him for the apartment he kept for her in Lyon, grateful that he would often come to stay with her. She talked about the opera and the plays they saw together, the fun they had at some friends' parties. Two of the letters were about the marvelous feeling of expecting a child from him, the following four about the sadness of a miscarriage. There was no mention of "that unfortunate situation with Valérie." The letters stopped during the war. Isabelle did not find any reference to any other kind of illness either. The recurrent theme was simply a statement of Justine's undying love for Edmond, expressed in beautiful lyric terms throughout her correspondence. Isabelle wondered how much of their time the two lovers had actually been able to spend together.

The second stack of letters, held together with a rose ribbon, was a collection of Edmond's letters to Justine. Romantic and poetic as well, they were however more explicative and Isabelle was thus able to understand some of the mysteries which had puzzled her so far. The "unfortunate situation" turned out to be the fact that Edmond's wife, Valérie, had been confined to a psychiatric hospital in Rodez almost from the beginning of their marriage. Not having a solid ground for divorce, he would have had to wait for his wife to die before he could marry Justine, and, apparently, the woman outlived Edmond. There was a melancholic letter, expressing his sadness at Justine's miscarriage, with the hope that they still could have a child, some day. There were also references to "a difficult mission" he was going to undertake and about which he could not give any details. He was asking Justine to be patient and to trust that everything would be all right. This was the last letter in the stack. How sad! Isabelle thought How very sad! Claire had pictured her sister as this pretty social butterfly, flaunting her lovely face and expensive clothes. Did she have any idea of what was happening in Justine's life?

Isabelle looked through a pile of small books. They were mostly spiritual readings. A life of St Thérèse, some "*pensées*" by Pascal and Teilhard De Chardin, and a small diary. "What kind of a butterfly would read such books?" Isabelle wondered, as she opened the diary.

Here was Justine's soul. She wrote of her love as something sacred but that everyone saw as evil doing. She expressed the pain of having to hide her feelings from her family most of the time, because they did not understand her. She even mentioned her sister's jealousy and how impossible it was to communicate with her. Justine revealed the hardship of being separated from Edmond when her heart longed for his presence, but not wanting to make his life more complicated by letting him know how lonely she felt. She described the solace she found in nature and the peace it brought to her solitude, the joy she experienced at playing with her cat.

Isabelle paused and felt the spider's thread from Justine to herself carrying love of nature and even, she chuckled, the cat. She read on.

> *I hold onto my dream of having a family with Edmond. Perhaps we could do as Monsieur Gauguin did and escape to an exotic island and live freely amongst the natives and palms. But in the meantime, I have made another lovely hat that I had the pleasure of wearing with my new silk frock. I can at least have fun to keep my heart in check while Edmond is engaged in his duties. And my stage play on the manners of the bourgeois is coming right along. Just writing it quite makes me laugh out loud sometimes.*

THE ENTRIES WERE WRITTEN as if Justine had recorded her passing thoughts, without dates, without sequence, simply noting down an idea when it happened, and there was no mention of an illness in the diary, which ended with this entry "I can't write anymore, it is too painful." In terms of events, it seemed to end about the time the letters ended."

Isabelle set the diary on the desk with a reverent touch. Claire talked so much about her struggles all of her life, and Isabelle didn't question that. Justine had struggled, in her own way, putting on a constant positive face and using her millinery talents, love of clothing, and writing to keep her spirits up.

Isabelle put the various relics back into the desk and rolled the top down. She locked it and walked downstairs. Claire was sitting in the park, under the linden tree, looking depressed.

"Here is the key, Mamie. I read some of Justine's papers."

They sat together quietly. Claire pressed the key into her palm.

"Did you know that her lover died during the war?"

"Yes. He recruited your father into his resistance unit. Marguerite was very upset about it. The whole outfit got caught the same day and later shot."

"Oh, Mamie, that's terrible."

"Edmond should have never talked your father into joining. He was so young, so idealistic. Edmond was bad news."

"It was the war, Mamie, and they wanted to save this country from the Germans. Wasn't this a noble cause?"

Claire shrugged. "Maybe."

"Can you tell me what Aunt Justine died of? A letter mentioned that she was ill."

"She died of TB, in a sanatorium… alone."

Isabelle's Dream

Isabelle started crying as she kneeled in front of her grandmother. For the loss of her father; for Justine's loss of Edmond; for Mamie's loss of her sister. "Aunt Justine's life ended in such a sad way!"

"Yes, and I never was able to talk to her. It was too late. The wall between us never came down." Claire was also crying, stroking Isabelle's head softly. Isabelle lifted her head. She had an inspiration as she looked at her grandmother's devastated face.

"Mamie, we must do something. You and I share this secret pain now and we must try to put Justine's memory to rest with something really special"

"Like what?"

"Let's burn the letters and the diary and free Justine's spirit so she can join Edmond with no threads tying her to the past. Let's forgive her and forgive you at the same time. Can we?"

"Yes, Isabelle, it would feel good, very good." Mamie looked at her granddaughter with a mystified expression on her face. "You are so different from everybody else, Isabelle. I don't understand. When I'm with you, everything becomes easy. I don't know how you think of these things to say and do. You fix things up, somehow. It's strange."

Isabelle laughed heartily. "It's probably because I'm from California."

That evening after dark Isabelle, Florence, and Mamie built a little fire in the middle of Pépé's old garden. Florence took Edmond's letters, Mamie held Justine's, and Isabelle opened the diary. In silence, they each slowly added pages until they burned all of Justine's letters and diary, that evening. The flames danced brightly in the night for a while, as the three women held hands, silently, letting the shadow spirit of the past fly up into the great mystery of the universe in light and heat and smoke and beauty.

"I'll turn these ashes into the soil," Florence said, "and plant a fall garden in honor of Justine."

Mamie nodded her approval and gave her caretaker a glance of thanks.

As the flames died down, Isabelle and Florence wheeled her grandmother back into the house, where they all went to bed with gratified hearts.

ISABELLE REFLECTED on the gifts she had inherited from her aunt Justine. In the morning before breakfast, she wrote in her own journal:

> *Like Justine, I am a pretty romantic woman who believes in love. Justine however, gave her lover great latitude to work with his duties and commitments. I have never done this in my love life. I have always clung tightly for fear of being abandoned. Perhaps this is why I lost these men*

> *I supposedly loved. Justine's strength was in her poetic, her spiritual, her romantic, and her creative side. It was in her deep appreciation of nature and also of beauty. If I can further develop this side of myself, I'll find the same strength. I have these qualities, too.*
>
> *I have been held back by the powerful negative snake energy: the sibling rivalry that always insinuates that someone else is better, that I am not good enough. That energy burned with the letters and diaries. It died when Claire had been able to spit her venom out. There is nothing standing in the way of my transformation, now. I will neither feel abandoned any more nor less of a person than anybody else. My sense of self has shifted along with my grandmother's revelation and change—within the spider's web.*

AS SHE PUT DOWN HER JOURNAL, a great peace fell over Isabelle. Suddenly she wanted to try out her new connectivity to Justine so she returned to the attic, looking for the hatbox. "There it is!" she said, reaching way back behind the trunk. It was a large round box filled with the most imaginative hats she had ever seen. When she saw the contents, Isabelle felt that a magical spring had been locked away in the box for years and it gushed to life in vivid hues of yellow, pink, pale green, and white. She sat on the attic floor and spread out the delightful creations that Justine had fashioned. Most of them were made of straw, some with large brims, others soft and floppy. Sometimes the brim was decorated with silk flowers. A white felt one had a gorgeous gold ribbon tied in a bow on the side After stroking them and gazing at them, Isabelle chose a pale pink straw cloche hat, adorned with a grey ribbon and silk flowers on one side. She pulled the pretty chiffon grey dress and the white lace shawl out of the trunk and brought the outfit down to her room.

Dressed in the grey dress, the shawl, and the pink straw hat, she gazed at herself in the full-length mirror with the greatest delight. They were a perfect fit. She stood in front of the mirror, making faces, admiring herself from all sides, smiling widely while she pirouetted. "This is what it feels like to be a butterfly," Isabelle exclaimed as she whirled around in chiffon waves.

"I must show Claire." And she ran down the stairs with great excitement. When her grandmother saw Isabelle, her mouth dropped.

"I don't believe this vision. Justine is alive all over again! You look so much like her, Isabelle, you just don't know."

"Mamie, thank you. That's a great compliment. Can I please take these clothes back with me to California? I feel like they are my new skin."

Mamie smiled so wide it pulled her wrinkles smooth and gave her a youthful glow. "Of course, Isabelle, take anything you want that belongs to Justine. Marguerite never wanted them. I guess they were just waiting for you."

"I only have two weeks left here." Isabelle sighed. "So little time—and to be honest I thought I was going to be a little bored. Little did I know, little did I know."

"I'm not in the grave yet, young woman. I can still light a few fires."

"You sure can, Mamie. You are a wildfire."

"Are you going to Clémentine's today?"

"Oh yes, I almost forgot. For tea this afternoon." Isabelle looked at Claire carefully, but this time her grandmother didn't seem to object. "To meet Philippe."

Mamie frowned and puckered her lips. "He is just as nutty as the rest of the family!" she said lightly with a twinkle in her eyes. "You'll see. He abandoned his country just like Marguerite did. What's so great about America, anyway?"

"It's a great place to live, Mamie. So varied and vibrant. I am sorry you've never visited it."

Mamie waved her hand dismissively. "I never want to go. You Californians are crazy. Your food is wretched. France is good enough for me."

"I understand Mamie. This is a stunning country, and you have a grand life."

VIII

The Smile

When Isabelle tapped on Victor's door, Philippe opened it wide with an inviting smile. He was not wearing a New York artist's black leather outfit but rather some faded Levis and a red t-shirt. Tall, slender like his grandfather, Philippe was in his late thirties perhaps, with high cheekbones, hazel eyes, and curly brown hair that came down his neck. Isabelle had expected him to be much younger and "nutty" looking—since that's what Claire had called him— so Philippe's appearance pleasantly surprised her.

"You must be Isabelle. I am Philippe," he said shaking her hand. "Please, come in. My grandparents are expecting you."

Isabelle walked into the dining room where the large table had been carefully laid with a pink tablecloth, a white china tea set, and silver spoons. Clémentine had made two different kinds of cookies and an apricot pie. Isabelle's azalea sat at one end of the table and gladiolas from the garden at the other end. The whole arrangement looked very festive.

"I feel very honored," Isabelle told Clémentine. "You've gone to so much trouble."

"Just an excuse for a party, Isabelle. Anyway, you know I love to bake and I am sure that Philippe won't mind."

"My grandmother knows I love her pastries. It's been a long time since I last tasted them."

"Three years, I believe," Clémentine said with mock disapproval.

He grinned and kissed her cheek. "What about you, Isabelle? When was the last time you were in France?"

"Three years, too. That's much too long, but this trip is making up for the lost time. I have gotten very close to my grandmother, something I never thought would happen."

"Did Claire finally talk about Justine?" Victor asked.

"Oh yes. After I returned from your house, the last time, we started to talk about Justine and that triggered a huge release in her. It was a wonderful moment for both of us, though I got worried for a while. She was sobbing and I couldn't stop her. But now Claire is feeling all right, and she talks freely about her sister. I am so happy it worked out this way."

"You must be some kind of a magician, Isabelle. The old lady is a tough cookie."

"Victor, don't talk about our neighbor that way," Clémentine scolded.

"I just meant she seems to be made of steel, rarely even gets sick. I'll stop by one of these days and check her blood pressure, just in case."

"We all should be that healthy," sighed Clémentine, bringing a steaming pot of tea to the table. "Come, sit down, and let's celebrate Philippe's visit."

Victor sat and quickly grabbed two cookies for his plate. Philippe pulled out his grandmother's chair. She sat down very gracefully and began to pour tea.

"And this is one of the reasons why I love to visit my grandmother," declared Philippe, holding up a cookie. "Not the only reason, of course, but a strong one. Being pampered is very good for the soul!" He took a big bite and murmured his pleasure.

Victor and Clémentine grinned from ear to ear as they ate and sipped tea with their eyes glued on the precious grandson.

"May I have a piece of your apricot pie, Mamie?" Philippe asked, handing his plate over to Clémentine "I haven't tasted it for a long time and it smells divine."

"Yes, it's the best, and you could have it here as often as you wished, bad boy who left his country!" Clémentine poked him. "Defector!"

Isabelle almost intervened to extol the virtues of American pies—New England apple pie and Southern pecan pies—but preferred to leave Clémentine to her opinion. Clémentine and Claire would have found some common ground here, she thought. I'll have to get them together.

"How long have you been in the States, Philippe?" Isabelle asked.

"About eleven years, now. I live in New York, in Tribeca."

"He's a painter, like Picasso," said Victor.

"I am a painter. But not like Picasso, nor anyone else for that matter." Philippe looked at his grandfather with a slight frown.

"What sort of painting do you do?" asked Isabelle

"Abstract paintings. More like Miro than Picasso. I've had a few collectors but for bread-and-butter, I sell pieces to realtors to decorate public buildings or expensive apartment houses."

Isabelle's Dream

"I admit I don't understand his paintings," Clémentine interrupted. "I have seen some photos of them. I love his colors but I wish he would paint some beautiful landscapes, like the impressionists did; that, I understand, like Monet's flowers."

"Mamie, I'll paint your garden for you. I can do that, too," Philippe added laughing.

There was a silence as everybody ate pastry and drank tea. It seemed to Isabelle as if each was simply sharing in the joy of being together, in that moment.

Then Victor spoke out in a loud voice that almost made her jump. "What does your socialite ex-wife think of you becoming well known? She might be surprised one of these days!"

Philippe looked at Isabelle quickly and then down at the crumbs on his plate. "I don't know. I haven't seen her since our divorce, three years ago."

Isabelle was startled by the abrupt harshness of the subject. It was clearly an old wound in the family. Clémentine saw the questioning look on Isabelle's face. "Philippe was married to a beautiful American woman he had met in Paris and they went back to New York together eleven years ago. It was her home town."

"New York took some getting used to. I grew up here in southern France with Victor and Clémentine."

"I've been to New York several times," said Isabelle, "but I'm always glad to get back to California."

"Caroline didn't help." Clémentine sniffed with indignation. "She didn't think he made enough money and he wasn't famous enough, so they got a divorce. Right, Philippe?"

"You make it sound pretty simple, but I suppose that's basically what happened," Philippe said, punctuating it with a crisp laugh. "New York taught me something that I hadn't realized when I was a student in the *Ecole des Beaux Arts* in Paris. I learned that money precludes love sometimes. Paris was protective; New York more of a battleground. But it's the place to be now, when it comes to modern art. I've come to enjoy it very much. I'm making it on my own terms. But, Isabelle, enough deconstructing my life, tell me something about yours."

Isabelle hesitated and took some tea while she thought. "Well, like you I spent my early childhood here and then left. I'm visiting my grandmother and putting together some missing pieces in my background." She chuckled. "Actually, I'm unraveling a dream in which I saw all the females in my lineage. They had something important to say but made me figure it out for myself."

"The best way, dear. The only way," added Victor.

"What do you do for work?"

"I'm a teacher in California. My mother was born in France and I was born here also after my father died in the Resistance. My mother took me to the States with her after she remarried an American. Voilà. As simple as that. I am very American but always looking over my shoulder at my French heritage."

Victor wiped some tea from his lips with the soft linen napkin. "Your family is always inside of you—where ever you are. But let's go out in the garden and see what Philippe might paint for Clémentine."

The four of them wandered out of the house and gathered along the garden fence. Philippe pointed at the tomatoes. "How about those, Grandmother? They are a fabulous color."

Clémentine pursed her lips and shook her head.

Victor pulled back some cabbage leaves to reveal a beautiful little red cabbage. "Now that's going to be tasty."

Clémentine shook her head again. "I want to put it on the wall, not eat it."

Isabelle caught the scent of mint and saw a lush patch near the water faucet at the edge of the garden. "Look at that mint, Clémentine. It's so green. I can smell it all the way over here."

Clémentine clapped her hands. "Perfect. After he paints them, I can pick a bouquet and dry it for tea. I'll hang the picture in the kitchen and think of Philippe every day."

"I'll get some paints in the village and do it over the next few days," said Philippe.

On their quest for the perfect botanicals, no one had noticed the dark clouds gathering in the west until the sun went behind a cloud.

"Isabelle, look," Victor said with mock seriousness. "Is it going to be a tradition? Shall we have a storm every time you come to visit? I don't know what this means. Do you?"

"It means I have to get going, right now. I might just make it home before the rain, like the last time."

"I can give you a ride," Philippe offered.

"A ride?"

"Yes, I have this wonderful steed. Have you ever had a ride on a motorcycle?"

"No, and I'm kind of leery about them, but," she glanced at the ominous sky, "I suppose if you're a careful driver."

"You'll love it, Isabelle. The Honda belongs to my friend who owns the garage. He always lets me use one of his motorcycles when I come to La Bâtie for a few weeks. It's a great machine. I'll get my helmet."

"Well, I guess I'm off." She kissed Clémentine on each cheek. "I think you're going to get a beautiful little painting."

"Next time tell me more about Claire's epiphany, Isabelle. I'm very curious," said Victor.

Isabelle felt a drop on her cheek. "I will. See you soon."

She saw Philippe straddling a white motorcycle in front of the house. He popped the helmet on her head and as he started the engine said, "Jump on behind me." It purred like a big cat and made her laugh.

"Here we go, Isabelle. Hang on."

Isabelle clung to Philippe for dear life as the Honda bounced over the uneven roads, but after she became used to the ups and downs, she forgot her fear and simply enjoyed his fit, muscular body. It felt quite good to be close to him. Some of that male magic crept slowly up her arms, and Isabelle tightened her hold, sensing the wonder of that moment. Her face was caressed by the wind, and she breathed in the energy of the approaching storm. Isabelle closed her eyes and relaxed against him. Philippe remained silent, as he cautiously brought the white horse closer to her destination. Isabelle wondered whether he could feel her thoughts.

Just before they turned into the last stretch, Philippe stopped the engine and turned to Isabelle. "Did you enjoy the ride? These country roads aren't the best."

"I never thought I'd enjoy riding on the back of a motorcycle, but it's a great feeling."

"Would you like to take a trip to the mountains with me, next week?" He smiled shyly. "Just to take a day off from your grandmother."

She paused and then agreed. "You're right. It wouldn't hurt a bit for me to get away. It's been a little intense."

"What about the day after tomorrow. I'll do most of Clémentine's painting and then let it dry before I put on the last layer. I'd like to leave early so we can have a whole day. I'll pick up another helmet for you at the garage. I bet Clémentine will pack us lunch."

Isabelle nodded and grinned. "I'm sure she will."

"Bring your bathing suit. We can stop by the *Lac d'Aiguebelette* for a swim."

"Sounds terrific. And we can speak English for a change."

Philippe put down the kickstand and walked Isabelle to the house. Claire was sitting in the garden when they approached the house. "What in the world, Isabelle! Did you really ride on that thing?"

"Yes, Mamie, it was a lot of fun. Philippe is going to take me for another ride to the mountains on Tuesday."

"Hello, Claire. Do you remember me?" Philippe said, reaching for her hand.

"Oh, I remember you! You used to scare my chickens when you were a little boy."

"I was hoping you'd forgotten. Where are the little critters, anyway? I can do a real mean dog imitation for them! Grrrrr."

"Hush, young man. I don't have any more chickens. But I'm concerned about that contraption. Don't you scare my granddaughter with your wild machine. Those things are dangerous, you know."

"I know, Claire, and I will be very, very careful, I promise. Now I must get back to my grandparents before the storm hits."

Philippe headed down the path to the motorcycle calling over his shoulder. "I'll pick you up Tuesday morning, Isabelle."

Claire watched him drive away and shook her finger in the air. "I told you that this guy was nutty, Isabelle, and I was right! You must be careful with him," Claire added, as Isabelle wheeled her grandmother back into the house. But Isabelle smiled. She liked Philippe's kind of nuttiness.

ISABELLE FELT STRANGE the next day. The upcoming trip with Philippe was unnerving. She told herself several times that this was just a casual acquaintance, that Philippe was at least ten years younger than she was, and that she was silly to even think of him in a romantic sense so quickly. She tried to convince herself that he had simply offered to take her on this little excursion because he wanted to enjoy his motorcycle and needed someone to share it, but she remembered the exquisite sensation of pressing her body against his. "Imagine a whole day of this," she thought, "and heaven knows what else. Well, Catharine," she conjured the image of her good friend, "here's the old romantic in me." She wondered how Catharine was doing right at that moment, perhaps hiding in a country windmill with a blond Dutchman? She'd get a kick out of Isabelle's wild ride.

Isabelle puttered around in the attic that afternoon, sorting through little relics and trying on more of Aunt Justine's wardrobe. They made her feel exotic but a little silly. She went to bed early, hoping that a long restful sleep would make the time go faster till the next morning. Of course, sleep was nearly impossible under the circumstances. She finally dozed off, though, after she told herself that the situation was actually very simple: tomorrow she just would live in the present, be herself, follow her intuition, and whatever happened, she knew she could handle it.

Isabelle opened her bedroom curtains to an unblemished blue sky the next morning, taking it as a good omen. It would be a perfect warm summer day. She tried to find something pretty to wear, wishing for a moment that Justine's grey dress and pink hat were suitable for a motorcycle ride. But, alas, she had to settle for some comfortable cotton slacks, a light blue t-shirt, and a sweater. She packed her bathing suit, a towel, and a small cosmetic bag in a daypack and ate her breakfast with Claire who observed her closely.

"You won't come back too late, now, Isabelle. I don't want to be worrying about you."

"It's okay, Mamie, I am a big girl, you know, and I can take care of myself, even with "nutty" people. I don't know exactly when we'll be back. Philippe is really a very responsible man and no longer the little boy who used to scare your chickens. Give him a chance. Everything will be all right and I'll see you tomorrow." Isabelle kissed Claire goodbye.

Philippe arrived exactly on time. Isabelle posted herself at the gate, shortly before eight, hanging her small backpack from the fence. She felt like a schoolgirl, escaping on an outing, excited to go away from home and on to some adventure. She was filled with a great sense of freedom. Philippe showed up fifteen minutes later, stopped the Honda, handed Isabelle a borrowed white helmet, and explained that Clémentine had packed a terrific lunch for them.

"One more thing, Isabelle: You'll discover very soon how to hold on. I could hardly breathe when I took you home, the other day. I know it was your first time and you were a little afraid, but soon you'll be a real pro at this."

"I am sorry, I didn't realize," Isabelle answered, blushing red-hot.

"Nothing to be sorry about." Philippe grinned at her impishly. "It was an inspiring squeeze, but today we're going to travel several hours and I need my full lung capacity. We won't have much of a conversation while we travel, I am afraid. It's nearly impossible to hear each other with the helmets on and the engine noise. If there is something important you want to communicate, just tap me on the shoulder and I'll stop."

"Okay. And I won't squeeze too hard if you don't go too fast."

"I won't. We have plenty of time. We'll head for Chambéry now and make our first stop there."

The ride to Chambéry was exhilarating: a moderate climb to the mountain pass *Le Col des Echelles*, through gorgeous unfolding green landscapes. The bike was so open and close to the ground that Isabelle could smell the grass and feel the morning dew lifting. She held Philippe's waist lightly and comfortably.

"I'll show you a great part of town," Philippe said as he parked near the cathedral. "The pedestrian section is delightful. Shall we go get coffee?"

While the morning sun illuminated the town center, they sat on the terrace of a large sidewalk café, ordered coffee and croissants, and watched the shoppers hurry to the outdoor market across the street.

"What would you like to do, Isabelle?" asked Philippe. "I have a few places in mind I want to show you, but maybe you have a special request?"

"Let's visit *Les Charmettes*. Rousseau lived there. His home is a museum now. He spent a few years of his life in the company of Madame De Warens, his older mistress and benefactor. I loved his novel *Julie, or the New Héloise*. It was so scandalous the Catholic Church outlawed it. Is the village very far from here?"

"Just a few miles, I believe. I've never been there. Let's do it, then we can take the road toward the *Chartreuse Massif*, I want to show you the greatest monastery in the world."

The road to *Les Charmettes* followed a terraced hillside into a lovely green valley. They found Rousseau's charming old brick home, which had become a museum with the authentic wallpaper, furniture, and decor from 1737. Isabelle and Philippe fell silent as they walked from room to room. It was very simple and very beautiful. Outside each window was a lovely flower garden or a perfect view of the mountains or an orchard. It seemed the ideal place of rest and inspiration for a philosopher. Isabelle read from the brochure that Rousseau had been weak and ill but exceptionally happy wandering the hillsides in the morning and reading all afternoon.

"Those were the gracious days," Philippe sighed as they walked out, "when an artist or a writer could consecrate himself entirely to his creativity without having to make a living. A generous patron, in this case an older woman like Madame De Warens, would support his career because she believed in him. Lucky Jean-Jacques."

"Is this a hint, Philippe?" Isabelle teased.

"Touché, Isabelle. Now it's my turn to blush. By the way, how old are you?"

"Just turned fifty in March, and you?"

"I'll be forty in November. Two difficult passages, aren't they? Anyway, Madame De Warens was at least twenty-five years older than Jean-Jacques; he used to call her "Maman."

"I feel sorry for artists these days. You have to struggle so hard to make it. The days of romantic patronage are over for good, although I'm told I am hopelessly romantic, too. Thank you for bringing me to this place, Philippe."

"When we lose our sense of the romantic, we should just cover our heads and never get out of bed." He took her arm and led her back toward the motorcycle. "I'm getting hungry. Let's head for the *Chartreuse Massif* now. There's a great place by the Guiers River for a picnic, if I can remember where it is."

The white motorcycle climbed noisily toward the *Col du Granier* pass, protesting the altitude, winding through magnificent chestnut trees, hedges and meadows, below some sharp rocky heights towering over a tiny village or shadowing a grassy hill on which cattle grazed. When they arrived in St. Jean D'Entremont, Philippe made a turn toward the Guiers Springs, four kilometers away.

After a short hike, they came to a cirque where the Guiers River dropped down in a spectacular fall from a cave halfway up the mountain and landed in a rocky bed, cool and beautifully clear. Isabelle and Philippe ran like joyful children toward the stream. They took their shoes off to cross the icy water, their feet paralyzed for a minute, then marvelously warm and tingling after they got out. They laid out their picnic next to a rock on the edge of the river.

Clémentine had prepared quite a spread: fresh French bread, some appetizing cold cuts, two kinds of cheese, little *cornichons*, Dijon mustard, grapes, walnuts, and some of her cookies. A bottle of Perrier and a thermos of tea completed the picnic. It was simple but so elegant. Isabelle ate with delight.

After they finished tea and dessert, they sat close to each other, quietly, not knowing how to fill the silence that suddenly rose between them. Isabelle remembered the promise she had made to herself: to live in the moment and to follow her intuition.

"I feel so happy, Philippe—the beautiful river, the mountains, being here with you. This is such a precious moment." She closed her eyes. "How good life is!"

"Yes, life is good. And as strange and rash as it might be, I think I'm falling in love with you," Philippe whispered. He pulled Isabelle gently into his arms and kissed her tenderly for a long time. Then he leaned back and looked over every inch of her face and smiled. "We've been teasing each other ever since we met. I guess it was because we immediately felt something strong. I'm so happy to be here with you."

Isabelle nodded and leaned into him, and the two remained silent, watching the river flow by their feet. She didn't want to move or speak or break the magic of the moment.

A fisherman forded the Guiers and walked past them. He smiled and said, "Beautiful day, isn't it?"

"Yes, yes, a beautiful day," Philippe answered, slowly releasing Isabelle. "I think we need to head up to the *Grande Chartreuse* now."

"It's not far from here. A great drive through the mountains. Enjoy your visit," the fisherman added as he walked along the bank toward a still eddy.

Isabelle and Philippe resumed their trip toward the *Grande Chartreuse*. They discovered the magnificent stone monastery in a pine forest at the foot of the *Chartreuse Massif*. It was entirely walled in, but they could see the upper part of the intricate complex: a harmonious composition of sober turrets with steep slate roofs and rows of the small cells where the monks resided, each one of the tiny dwellings topped by a chimney. The monks spent their time in prayer but they also walked far into the mountains to gather wild herbs and flowers that were part of the famous Chartreuse recipe. It was a secret blend for a yellow-green liquor, originated centuries ago and now known all around the world. Silence was the rule around the premises inspiring visitors to whisper the minute they entered the sacred grounds. Isabelle and Philippe held hands as they walked toward the *Correrie*, a museum replica of the interior of the monastery that was off limits. There were some eloquent pictures of the simple monastic life, reproductions of a monk's cell and a small chapel where recorded Gregorian chants diffused a strange mixture of celestial peace and beauty, giving Isabelle a vision of another life without modern concerns, the noise of civilization, and the pollution of the soul. Under an inspiring picture of a group of tall trees, casting their shadows on a sunlit forest, there was this quote by Aug. Guillerand:

We are larger than ourselves and this is why we suffer inside,

We are large as God is, but only if we enter him.
There is only one thing that matters; it is the instant which passes,
it is the present moment,
It is the infinite love that God put in each of these moments.

PHILIPPE AND ISABELLE had not said a word since they had entered the sanctuary, but their hands had gently tightened or released, speaking the deep emotion they felt. As they walked back to the parking lot, Philippe said. "The last time I visited this place, Isabelle, I started feeling the weight of my human condition so intensely the minute I left that I almost became depressed." He stroked a strand of hair away from her forehead. "But today I'm happy. My spirit is soaring. I guess falling in love is also an experience in transcendence."

"What do you mean by transcendence?"

"The need to get beyond the self and into another. Today I feel so light, Isabelle." He paused, looked away, and then looked back at her. "I know it seems too quick to say it but I do love you."

She knew he was taking a great emotional risk and deserved an answer. "Words can't quite convey what I feel, Philippe. Bliss, perhaps. It's all right to say it: I love you, too. Here, in this place, it seems sacred. Do you know what I mean?"

"I do," he whispered and pulled her close. Philippe and Isabelle leaned against the monastery's stonewall and hugged. They listened to each other's heartbeat and their lips joined softly.

Philippe suddenly squeezed her tight and lifted her off the ground. "And now, for a down-to-earth treat. Let's go swimming, Isabelle. The human condition can be a wonderful state after all, don't you think?"

Her laugh was like a bubble of water hitting the surface of a pond. "Oh yes."

When they reached the *Lac d'Aiguebelete*, it was late in the afternoon. The lake was as still as a mirror and the sun had started its descent. They rented a boat and rowed for a while next to a family of ducks. They glided across the water, laughing, joking, splashing each other like rascals. They docked the boat in a sheltered cove out of sight of the dock. On a soft bed of grass, they abandoned themselves to a sacred earthly transcendence they had brought from the monastery, merging into one and releasing themselves to love, so hard to find, yet which moves the world.

Just before the sun set, they swam in the warm lake water, in naked freedom, relaxed and joyous. Later, Isabelle felt ravenously hungry and suggested that they eat dinner at a small restaurant they'd passed on the edge of the lake. Philippe gently rowed them back toward the dock.

"Do you know a poet named Lamartine?" Philippe asked. Isabelle shook her head. "He wrote of an evening when he was rowing his lover in a boat, on Lake Bourget, and he wanted to eternalize the moment:

O time, suspend your flight! And you, happy hours,
suspend your race:
Let us savor the fleeting delights of our fairest days.

"WHY IS IT THAT WE ALWAYS WANT to stop within the blissful moment as if we're afraid that it'll never return? Is it that moments of ecstasy are so short that we want to cling to them?" His gaze looked sad in the evening shadows. "But it's the clinging which stops the flow, isn't it? And love is flowing, like a river, like life itself."

"You're so different from any man I have ever known, Philippe. So tender. So present."

"When I decided to become an artist, it was partly to allow these kinds of feelings all the time. I don't want to hold back, ever."

Isabelle reached out to touch his hand on the oar. "You never have to hold back with me."

IT WAS ALMOST DARK when they arrived at the restaurant. They were very hungry—from love, sun, swimming, and intensity. They tasted local fresh fish with a green salad and drank a glass of white wine, toasting their unanticipated romance.

Philippe looked over the water, which caught the glimmer from the restaurant lights. "This exquisite day is almost over. I'd like to spend more time with you, a few days. Could you get away? I could rent a car and we could drive to the South of France together. I have a friend there who would let me use his summer place in the country."

"I would love to, Philippe, but I won't be able to stay very long. My flight leaves in two weeks and I'll have to give Claire an excuse for leaving her."

"What does a week sound like, Isabelle? We could leave Thursday and come back the following Wednesday evening. You'd still have three days before and after to spend with your grandmother before you left."

Isabelle's Dream

"I'll try, Philippe. There is nothing I'd like more." She sipped her wine, savoring its gently dry bite. "Being with you is as delicious as this *vin de table*."

They straddled the white motorcycle and headed through the mountains back to La Bâtie. She hugged him intimately, her head resting on his back, warmth radiating through her whole body. Midway through the trip, she tapped on his shoulder. Philippe stopped the Honda.

"I suddenly wanted to tell you this... Philippe, I love you."

He kissed her deeply under the stars with the dark Alps blessing their passion.

IT WAS TEN THIRTY when they finally arrived at La Bâtie. Philippe stopped the engine at the gate. Isabelle tiptoed quietly into the house but found Claire waiting for her, seated in the dining room, straight up, a small candle burning dramatically on the table.

She scowled into the little flame. "Where have you been, Isabelle? Why did you come home so late? I was worried about you. What did you do with this man?"

"I... I'm sorry. I didn't mean..." Isabelle, torn from her marvelous feeling of that perfect day, started to think of some excuses and apologies but, all of a sudden, the irony of the situation overwhelmed her. Here she was, being treated like a little girl and asked to give an account of her whereabouts. She grabbed her grandmother's hands and started to laugh, so hard that she couldn't stop.

"I don't think it's funny, Isabelle. I was sitting on hot coals waiting for you."

"But, I think it's funny, Mamie, because you're talking to me as if I were fifteen years old. I am fifty, Mamie, fifty. I don't need to apologize for my behavior, and if you want to know, Philippe made love to me by the lake. He is a wonderful lover and I am going to the South of France with him for a week. I am very, very happy. Now, you and I are going go to bed. Am I still your favorite granddaughter, though?"

Claire seemed disarmed by Isabelle's reaction. She looked at her granddaughter's radiant face, sighed loudly, then said in a resigned tone, "You are just as romantic as Justine—and just as shameless. Here I was, imagining the worst while you were doing... I can't even say the words."

"Now you know, nothing bad happened, and next time you'll realize I'm a grownup and take very good care of myself. Good night, Mamie. I love you."

Mamie now smiled in the soft candlelight. "Good night, naughty child. You have a wicked way to twist me around your finger, I must say, but I love you, too."

Isabelle blew the candle. "You have a great sense of drama, Mamie. You looked like you were waiting for death to come and get you, sitting up in that semi-dark room."

Mamie looked up at her. Her old eyes were deep pools. "It won't be long, Isabelle. It won't be long."

ALL THE EXCITEMENT OF THE DAY subsided as Isabelle started up to her room, climbing the stairs slowly with a vision in her mind: Claire sitting in the darkness of the dining room, her stern wrinkled face barely lit by the burning candle, and repeating, "It won't be long." Isabelle's mood became sad as she felt a rush of love for the tender old woman. Perhaps Claire was not this paragon of strength she appeared to be, and Isabelle had made her face some pretty difficult situations in the past few days. Perhaps she would not live long. Perhaps?

Isabelle felt she had gone too far. She ran her fingers through her hair then sat on the bed for a long time, trying to figure out what to do, She finally fell asleep around one and woke up at four. I guess it is afternoon in California, she thought. She sat up abruptly. "I'll call Mom. That's what I'll do." She tiptoed down the stairs to the old phone in the hall.

After a few rings Marguerite answered, "Allo."

"Mother, how are you?"

"Isabelle? What's going on? Nothing bad I hope. Tell me, how is Claire?"

"She's okay, don't worry. We're having a great time and revealed a lot of problems about her relationship with Justine, but although she seems to take things in stride, she's worried about me and… "

"I hope you didn't do anything crazy, Isabelle. Why is she worried?"

Isabelle suddenly felt embarrassed and, well, almost adolescent. "I met this guy and I fell a little in love."

"Here we go again."

"No, it's not like that. I'm different. I'm having fun. We're going to go on a trip in a couple days."

"No wonder she's worried. Who is he?"

"Do you remember Victor and Clémentine?"

"Yes, the doctor and his wife. A little weird, but not as bad as Californians." Marguerite laughed.

"He's their grandson."

"Oh yes. Philippe. Right? But wait, he's pretty young as I remember."

"I'll explain later, but I have a favor to ask you, a big favor."

"Okay, lay it on."

"Could you come a little earlier than you planned? Claire seems kind of tender and open and might need you while I am away. You two can talk, and you can meet Philippe when we get back."

"So this is it. You want me to baby sit Claire while you're having fun. That's quite a request, Isabelle." Marguerite was silent for a few minutes. Isabelle knew better than to push her. If her mother didn't want to do something, you could beg until the cows came home and it would be useless. "Let me see what I can do," Marguerite said in her problem-solving voice. Isabelle cheered silently. "Actually, Naomi could tend the store for me, but what about the ticket? I'll call right away and arrange things. What time is it in La Bâtie?"

"About 4:30. I'll go back to sleep now that I know you're coming. I feel so much better. Thank you, Mom, thank you, thank you, thank you."

"Be careful Isabelle. You've had enough bad luck with men."

"Don't rub it in, Mom. I know, but this time it's different."

"Famous last words! Good night, Isabelle."

"Thanks again, Mom, you're an angel."

"I'll call in a couple of days with my new travel schedule."

ISABELLE WENT BACK UPSTAIRS. Did Claire ever have anything exciting like this happen to her? she wondered. This marvelous glowing feeling of knowing that someone deeply loves you— the tingling skin, the overflowing heart, the bliss which invades every cell, bathing you in a pool of warmth. Isabelle had not tasted these feelings for a long time and she'd never experienced them so strongly. "This must be a fringe benefit of getting older?" she wondered with a sleepy chuckle. No time to waste. Perhaps it becomes easier to taste the moment, let the spirit bypass the mind and simply let it guide you. Isabelle went into deep sleep with a smile on her face. "Remember, remember," whispered a voice in her dream.

ISABELLE OCCUPIED HER NEXT DAYS preparing for the trip and spending some time with Claire. Even though she told her grandmother that Marguerite was coming soon, Mamie roamed around the house like a lost soul.

Philippe stopped by with a rented car to finalize the details about their escape. They sat together outside the house and Isabelle told him about Mamie's sadness and her mother's plans.

"My grandparents were pretty surprised, too. But after they thought about it—and I think gossiped about us between themselves—they thought it actually was nice that we're together."

Together. Isabelle liked the soft, easy sound of that.

"Clémentine had even added 'This girl needs to get rid of a curse. I hope you can help her.' What's the curse?"

Claire rolled her chair to the door, wanting to come out but too embarrassed and shy. Philippe jumped up and pushed her next to them by the garden. She looked at them and then away several times, like she wanted to say something but couldn't.

"Well," said Philippe with a grin at Isabelle. "I'd better get home."

The two women sat together quietly.

Isabelle finally broke the tension. "Mamie, I know something's on your mind. You usually don't hesitate. What's up?"

"I want to tell you something, Isabelle. I've never told anyone about this and I don't know why I should tell you this, but I feel that I would like to tell you. I think I would, at least, because I…"

"What is it, Mamie? You know we don't have any secrets from each other anymore."

"Okay. You're very modern or I wouldn't dream of…" she twisted a little handkerchief into a knot. "When I was almost your age I had an affair."

"How wonderful!"

Mamie put up her hand. "Don't ask me any details, it just happened. Pépé was sick and it was my only joy. I have been so ashamed of it that I could never bring myself to talk about it."

Isabelle was dying to know the details but checked her eagerness in deference to the older woman's fragile breakthrough. "I'm glad you've said something. I don't think you're horrible."

"It made me feel so good and so bad at the same time. I envy your freedom, Isabelle, and I want to wish you the best."

"We've become each other's confidant and friend. Imagine, we've shattered the long held secrets that didn't make anybody happy." Isabelle took the hankie out of Mamie's hands and held the gnarled fingers in her palms. "It's the most beautiful gift you could have ever given to your granddaughter. Thank you."

Isabelle's Dream

Isabelle kissed her grandmother affectionately. "Now how about an extra long foot massage."

Mamie smiled. "Ah, yes. I bet Marguerite won't give me one."

Isabelle shrugged, thinking probably not, but she said, "You never know how people are going to change. It seems to happen at any age."

IX

White Lace

After putting her suitcase on the back seat, Isabelle sat in the Peugeot, her heart racing. Philippe looked at her, with a soft glow in his eyes. She was wearing comfortable slacks and a blue silk blouse with Justine's lovely white lace shawl over her shoulders. He leaned over and kissed her cheek.

"We're getting away again, Isabelle, but this time I won't need to tell you to hang on."

"I love to hug this wonderful chest of yours, as you've very well noticed, Monsieur Philippe. I'm looking forward to this ride even more than the motorcycle adventure, though, because now we can talk."

Philippe chuckled and started the engine. "We have a long ride ahead, long enough to get to know each pretty well. I feel that I've already discovered the essential part of you: your soul. But there are probably a few things left to learn."

"Absolutely. I'm like a thousand-page novel. What would you like to know?"

"Let's see. I know. What is that hint my grandmother made about a curse?"

"That's a long story, Philippe."

"It's a long drive."

Isabelle half turned to her lover, put her head on his shoulder, then leaned back and gazed at him seriously. "I have always felt insecure with men, Philippe. I felt deeply unsettled and would cling to them. Why did I think they would abandon me? Now I am starting to see it as a pattern."

"And you would set yourself up for the very outcome you feared."

"Yes, of course. With George, my last lover, I was always watching him and questioning his whereabouts and imagining he would want another woman in his life just because I wasn't good enough. When I realized he really wanted his drinks more than me, I was devastated."

"Is the fear gone now?"

Isabelle gazed out at the lush summer countryside and nodded gently. "Yes, it is. The 'curse' is that women in my background experienced and played out these deep uncertainties and jealousies in their lives without ever being open about them. I hope that by asking my grandmother to face her jealousies and fears, I'm resolving it for both of us."

"When did you start breaking the curse, as you call it?"

"I guess it began with Georges. He's an alcoholic. I tried to make it work in spite of his drinking, but he didn't want to give up the stuff. For a long time I was afraid to leave him and I kept hoping for the best, but I finally found the strength to give him an ultimatum: booze or me. Not harshly, though. I tried to do it without fury, with a little grace so I'd feel good about myself. That was my last relationship, and I broke it off just before I started on this trip."

"I can't see you catering to an alcoholic who doesn't want to change. Your spirit is too strong to be wasted like that."

"Thank you, Philippe. The spirit was there, but spider webs hid my true self from emerging as being good. I always compared myself to others and my mother didn't help with her disapproval. I now think her disapproval was part of the threads connecting us all to this family sadness and incompleteness. She had her own abandonment memories from the war. Anyway, this is now old stuff."

"I find it intriguing. It's the evolution of so many women at once."

Reassured by Philippe's acceptance of her as an evolving spirit, Isabelle continued her story. Including the dream that had prompted her to look for clues to hers and her mother's past by coming to La Bâtie for a few weeks.

"Your grandfather has been great. He knows my family well and his guidance led me to discoveries about my grand aunt Justine. I identify with her a lot. There was a big rivalry between her and Claire I didn't know about, which explains the ermine part of the dream. Claire was envious of Justine's elegance and freedom. Also, there were other women who were abandoned by their young husbands in the war—meaning they were killed. I love these unknown women who were in my bloodline, and I've found a way to Claire's heart, the one hiding behind her armor."

"That is a feat in itself, Isabelle!" Philippe exclaimed, laughing, "You should have seen how she scared me and my friends when we were kids." He paused thoughtfully. "But I always tried to get close to her; I knew it was all bluff."

"I'm sure it was. Anyway, Philippe, this trip to La Bâtie has given me a much clearer picture of the origins of my patterns, and that's what your grandmother called the 'bad fairy curse': abandonment, compounded by some 'resonances' as Victor puts it, of an old sibling rivalry in the family, and this damned sense of not being good enough."

"I admire the way my grandparents are able to put into simple language such obvious solutions to difficult problems. Their level of psychological sophistication was way ahead of their time even if they never expressed it as Freudian or Jungian."

"Do you want to hear about the good fairy's part?"

"There is a good fairy, too?" He grinned, showing a small gap between his two front teeth. She kissed him playfully.

"The good fairy is a happy one, eh?" He put his hand on her thigh. "She gave you a great body as well as a deep soul."

"Watch out or we'll have to pull over right now."

"Or wait until we're under a feather quilt."

"That sounds so nice. Drive on." Isabelle picked his hand up, turned it over, and kissed Philippe's hand. She leaned back and continued the saga of her encounters with Justine's life, including the visit to the attic, the discovery of her letters and diary, Claire's catharsis, and the ritual burning of Justine's relics with her grandmother.

"I feel such a strong kinship with Justine, with her creative, romantic, and spiritual nature. I share Justine's vision of love as sacred. It isn't just about men; it's a truly encompassing love, embracing Nature and Beauty." She put her head back on the seat and closed her eyes.

"My God, Isabelle. What an emotional summer. Aren't you exhausted?"

She looked at him under half-open lids. "I've never felt better in my life. The fire that has sparked this growth had been smoldering for a long time. It just needed a flash of French spirit to ignite it and take off like wild fire. It's a special gift for my 50th year. Justine died in her fifties and I'm only now starting to live fully. It's so strange. Why did I have to wander in the spider web forest for so long?"

"You're an evolving woman, Isabelle. We all can if we're willing to do the hard, uncomfortable work around it. It can be the hardest task of our lives. The uncertainty, harsh truths, and recognition of wasted time in a finite life are so painful. I know. I've had my own mountains to climb, too."

"Like Sisyphus?"

"I am not so sure that Sisyphus was that self-aware. He never stopped pushing his rock long enough to gaze at the Earth from the top of the hill—and why in the world did he have to push the damn thing anyway? I prefer to climb with an ice pick, then I stop on the summit, enjoy the reward of my efforts, and admire the view for a while."

"Will you tell me about your spider webs, Philippe?"

"I will, after we stop for lunch. I'm starved, Isabelle."

THEY WERE ABOUT TO REACH the town of Valence, halfway to their destination. There was an invisible but sensual border along the Rhône, and by the time they crossed it into the city, they looked at each other with expressions of gently awareness.

"Something's different," whispered Isabelle.

Philippe cocked his head. "The quality of light, perhaps."

"It's warmer."

"I smell eucalyptus and pine."

"It's making me hungry."

"Where to, Isabelle? A country inn, a brasserie, a sidewalk café, MacDonald's?

"Find the most French place in town."

They drove slowly down a boulevard around a park with a gazebo in the center. Philippe turned down a narrow side street and parked in front of a small stone hotel with a restaurant next to it. A waiter invited them in with much *joie de vivre* and brandished two large menus more fitting of a five star place. Philippe sat across from her and whispered, "Let's each have a little glass of Château Grillet. I know we still have to drive but it's one of the best wines of this region."

She nodded. Philippe waved the waiter back and ordered the wine and an artichoke with a parsley sauce, a crayfish gratin, some cheese and bread and a bottle of Badoit mineral water. Isabelle chose some eggplant Provençale and grilled sole.

They ate quietly, making pleasant small talk, resting from their deep conversation. "I'll drive," Isabelle said when they walked out of the restaurant. She held her hand out for the keys. "You can relax and I'll listen."

He tossed her the keys and arched his back. "All right, but let's take a walk in the park to stretch a little. My back is stiff."

They strolled around the gazebo and a pool with fountains. Philippe drew her down on a bench where they hugged and kissed each other tenderly, forgetting time and space, as well as the passersby who glanced at them with understanding, perhaps envious, smiles.

Philippe became a little breathless. "I can't wait to hold you in my arms, again, Isabelle."

"Soon, my Romeo, soon." She stood up. "Come, let's keep going so we don't have to wait too long." She grabbed his hand and they ran back to the car like two adolescents on a lark.

Shortly after they left Valence, a humming noise began to build all around the countryside.

"Cicadas. This means we're getting close to the south. They'll be our constant companions, now, as long as it's warm outside. For me, this sound has always meant summer, intense heat, and walking alone in a parched landscape. From now on, it will remind me of you and of our trip together. It will be a love song."

Isabelle listened to the hum, letting it sink deep into her cells to call upon later when she was far away from this landscape and his presence.

"My spider webs have been hard to see through, Isabelle. It was only after the pain of my divorce that I began to understand some of my background 'resonances.'"

"What's the source of your pain? Besides your disappointment in marriage?"

"Basically, I'm afraid of being successful. On one hand, I want it; on the other hand, I'm afraid to achieve it and often sabotage myself in the process. I was brought up with two siblings, in a very conventional family, where I was expected to fit the mold. From way back, the men on both sides of my family had been successful lawyers, businessmen, doctors, and politicians. They all achieved wealth and status. My siblings were good students and followed the path. I didn't."

"You're an artist."

"I can't escape it—ever. When I was a little boy, I already had an artistic nature, even though my family belittled my constant painting and drawing and writing. But it's my calling. I kept at it no matter how derisive they were—that's how I knew I had no other choice.

"I managed to go to art school against all odds and met Carol, my now ex-wife, later in Paris. She was an American and leaving my country to follow her wasn't difficult. It was liberating." He looked at Isabelle shyly. "Carol was quite beautiful and I was very much in love with her. Unfortunately, her Bohemian facade wore off quickly. She was very conventional and her values were upper crust. Carol became disenchanted by my vocation—which had appealed to her, as long as she could show me off to her New York friends, introducing me as 'my husband, the artist.' We went to parties, stayed at her parents' estate on Long Island, traveled to the Bahamas, and lived high on the hog for a few years. I tried to stay with my painting, though I couldn't sell much of my work at first.

"Carol began to unload her expectations on me: I was not successful enough: I was not making enough money, we couldn't afford to do all the things her friends were doing. Things disintegrated between us and she asked for a divorce. I went through hell for a long time, feeling guilty, responsible, unable to understand the whole picture. I felt so small."

Philippe stopped talking, frowning as if he were reliving this chaotic period of his life.

"But what about Victor, your grandfather? He seems so very different from these other relatives."

"That's my 'good fairy' part of the story, Isabella. Victor is my father's dad, and though he became a physician himself, he never fitted the mold either. He never gave up his soul. I think Clémentine contributed for a good part to this miracle. Victor was my mentor, in a way."

"Like Justine was for me."

"His love of Nature, his witty mind, his acceptance of living a simple healthy life in a small town away from society's demands—even being labeled "nutty" didn't seem to faze him or Clémentine. Probably because of them, I've learned to accept myself as successful. Keeping my soul intact is what counts. It's a lifelong process, but I have a great sense of freedom these days, and am following my intuition more and more. Turning forty is a new challenge, though. I have things I must accomplish for myself." He stroked her arm. "We're both at turning points, Isabelle."

"I'm at a turning point for good, this time," Isabelle declared with a smile that lit her whole face.

Their intimacy filled the little Peugeot as they drove through the Rhone valley. Isabelle felt the embrace of fertile orchards and vineyards. Philippe put his arm around her shoulder and kissed her neck, tenderly, soothingly.

"Stop or I'll drive off the road, rascal. We're coming to Avignon soon and I'm not sure where to go."

He gave her a small playful bite and reached for the map in the glove box. "My friend's house is near the village of Gordes. I'll recognize my way when we get there, but turn ahead onto D22 East, and after you cross the N100 take D2 left. Simple enough?"

Philippe located Pierre's vacation home easily. He had already been there a few times. Pierre was a friend he had met at the Ecole Des Beaux Arts in

Paris, an artist, like himself. The key was waiting at the neighbor's house, and everything went magically well. Pierre had even phoned the neighbor to prepare the house for them and to stock the refrigerator.

Isabelle stared at the wines on the counter, fruit in a large basket, a large baguette, and cheese and salad in the fridge. "You have quite some friends, Philippe. This is a tremendous reception from an absentee host!"

"Pierre spent a month with me in New York, last spring. He was hoping I would take advantage of his place sometime, and I am going to do just that." Philippe lifted Isabelle in his arms and carried her toward the bedroom. "But I'm not hungry for food right now."

He laid her across the down comforter with a gentle bounce.

"Look at this giant bed. It's much larger than Madame De Warens's," Isabelle said, rolling over the covers. "Did you notice how small that was?"

"Of course I did, of course."

"I thought that they must not have had much of a sex life. Come closer, Philippe."

"Me too. But we were still too inhibited to talk about such things at the time. Are all of your inhibitions gone now, Isabelle?"

"It's so delicious being here with you," Isabelle whispered, as she abandoned herself to her lover.

X

The Kick

At first, the airline didn't want to change the date of her ticket on such a short notice. All flights were booked and Marguerita was put on a waiting list. As she packed, she kept asking herself why she had agreed so quickly to Isabelle's request, and all this because her daughter was on to another romance. Had she always accommodated Isabelle that way? Is that what her daughter had learned from her: accommodate, accommodate? No wonder she got into trouble with men. Yet the answer had come from her heart so spontaneously. Marguerite knew deep down that she would always be there for this only child she had raised with love and great hope, her only daughter who was not a child anymore. Love does not lie, but... what's next? She sighed.

The answer came as "a good omen" when the airline called and all of a sudden everything flowed smoothly: ticket change, Naomi's readiness to take over during her absence at the shop, a ride to the airport in comfort and plenty of time.

After a sleepless night—she never could rest on an airplane so she carried the longest novel she could find—she arrived in Paris under a cloudy sky. In front of Gare de Lyon, she stretched out her aches and pains from the flight and then raced to catch her train. Finally relaxing on the bus to La Bâtie, she gazed at the familiar landscape unrolling in the sunshine before her eyes and began to anticipate her arrival at her mother's house.

The last visit had not been the greatest, she recalled, frowning. Would Claire's old jealousy about Justine surface again and spoil Marguerite's memories of her beloved aunt? Would Claire bring up that old story about her young husband, why he had joined the resistance because of Justine's husband and his influence? Why Marguerite, then, had "rushed" to marry an American and leave France with her precious granddaughter Isabelle? Claire could so often be cold, judgmental, and even aggressive at times. Marguerite realized that blaming was a way for her mother to handle grief she felt about life. But it still made Marguerite nervous.

Leaving her suitcase at the café, Marguerite walked up the hill along the familiar route to her mother's house. She realized Isabelle had done the same just a couple of weeks earlier and she was comforted by many unchanged features of the village, the farms, the meadows, the homes and textile factories, the old trees. This landscape was written deep into her memory. She smiled and walked a little faster to the rhythmic sound of the clattering mills.

Home. There it was. Her heart beat fast as Marguerite opened the gate and walked into the alley. The door swung open and Florence came running toward her.

"*Bonjour, Florence, comme je suis contente de vous voir!*"

"I am so happy to see you too, Marguerite. Come, your mother is waiting for you inside," she exclaimed. "She just finished her lunch."

Marguerite walked into the dining room bathed in sunlight. Claire was sitting by the window in her wheeled chair, straight and composed, all dressed in black as usual, an inquisitive look on her face as if she were waiting for her daughter to make the first move in order to ease her own reserve.

Marguerite kissed her mother on both cheeks. "*Bonjour*, Mamie, you look great. Life agrees with you these days. I am happy to see you look so well."

The tension in Claire's face softened and she returned the kisses.

"You had a good trip, I hope."

"Yes, it was as easy as an international flight can be. At first, it was a hassle to change my plans. But here I am and it feels good."

"Isabelle conned you into coming and staying with me while she's having a fling with this nutty guy."

"Well, Mamie, I wouldn't put it that way. Isabelle is a mature woman and she knows what she's doing."

"Let's go to the garden. Could you push me, please?" Mamie added, "She's actually very dear. We've had a great time together. You raised a good kid, Marguerite." She smiled back at her daughter. "Though you could have done better if you'd stayed in France."

"And what do you mean by 'better', Mother?" Marguerite bristled.

"Oh, relax, I'm teasing. However, Isabelle could have married a French man, had kids and been here for me to see her grow up. You know… and I wouldn't have minded having you closer, too. I never liked the fact that you moved to America, but… "

"Let's not go into that again, Mamie. Besides, I sort of wish Isabelle had married and had kids in America. Unfortunately, that doesn't have anything to do with the country you live in. Life is what it is, no matter where you end up being. Right?"

Isabelle's Dream

"The garden is beautiful, isn't it? Florence and Isabelle have taken good care of it. Now that I see you in the sunlight, you look a little weary, Marguerite. Why don't you go up to your room and take a nap. Florence will drive to the café to pick up your suitcase. We can continue our visit later. We have plenty of time. I'm happy you are here."

Puzzled by how soft Claire seemed, Marguerite answered, "I'm happy to be here, too, Mamie"

Walking upstairs, Marguerite put her hand on the banister and memories flooded her whole body. Her childhood was there, in her hand, cradling the wood, all in one bundle of feelings She remembered running upstairs at five years old to meet Justine in her room, who would read her stories. Then her mind's eye saw her grandfather in his bed when he was sick and she hugged him goodnight. She smelled the camphor her grandmother rubbed on her sore joints, the rose water Justine splashed on her clothes. She looked up and saw the attic door, closed by a wood plank that matched the ceiling, and felt the promise of what hid inside. She felt like she was in a dream world and she let herself slip into it fully, away from time. It was strange, sensual, perfect.

"Is that what home really is?" she whispered. Yes, home. Is this what makes one feel so good? The familiar? The unchanged? As if you felt that life would go on forever.

Marguerite opened the door to her old bedroom, the one she shared with Germaine as a child. The shutters were closed. The twin beds were made up perfectly without a wrinkle like bunks in an army barrack. But pink sheets folded over the soft blankets and gleamed in the semi darkness. Hers was the bed on the right, the one next to the night stand which had a little cupboard where the night pot stood when there was no toilet in the house and no one wanted to run to the outhouse in the night. Germaine and she always fought to decide who would empty the pot in the morning. Marguerite laughed at the thought. On the table next to the window, the old porcelain washbowl still rested, with the water pitcher inside, a decoration now, holding pink and white flowers instead of clean water. The hand mirror, with its silver frame, lay sleeping next to the bowl. How many of the girls' changing faces had it reflected? The armoire was still there, waxed and shiny; the rug at the end of the beds was elegantly worn. Nothing had changed.

In spite of its slightly musty smell, the room felt good. Marguerite opened the shutters and the window to let the air come in, stretching in delight at the view of the mountains in the distance. She was home, she felt happy.

She pulled down her covers, lay in the cool sheets, closed her eyes, and fell asleep immediately and deeply.

It was almost dinnertime when Marguerite came back downstairs. Claire was waiting for her.

"Florence picked up your suitcase; it's in the hall. Did you have a good sleep?"

"Very good, Mamie, I dreamed about picking cherries in the park and you were walking around telling us to leave some on the tree for the next day. Weird, isn't it? I guess you have always been thinking about saving food. Something you learned during the war!"

"I'd rather forget those hard times. We did what we had to do."

"I will never forget. Even my dreams remind me of it. By the way, did Isabelle tell you about that dream she's trying to understand?"

"Not exactly, but I know she's been poking around in old papers, in trunks in the attic, and she talked to Victor about heaven knows what old family stories. She asks very indiscreet questions, you know. Did you raise a little detective?"

"What kind of questions?"

"Mostly things about Justine and about a snake next to her ermine scarf. Very strange."

"Were you able to answer her questions?"

Claire chuckled. "Isabelle has a way to twist you around and make you say things you did not want to talk about. It's a bit like going to confession and telling the truth to the priest because you feel guilty but don't know why. She is very clever, that girl. I'd forgotten how angry I was about the scarf which Justine paraded in front of my friends at the office." Mamie's voice began to rise but she paused and took a deep breath. "To be honest, I see things differently because of what Isabelle said. Clever, very clever…" Claire repeated, with a puzzled look on her face. "We've became good friends, you know. I love that little detective. She even made me cry."

Marguerite was speechless. She had expected a litany of criticism from Claire about Justine, as usual, yet she was now facing a woman accepting a difficult memory, who seemed very peaceful about it. How did Isabelle manage to make her change so much, she wondered.

"So you feel all right about Justine, Mamie, but still resentful about my leaving France with Isabelle?" Marguerite threw spitefully at her mother.

Claire looked puzzled. "I suppose I do. You know, in Isabelle's dream you kicked the snake and it rose up all dark and menacing. What was that?

"I... I'm not sure."

"Dinner is ready," announced Florence, walking into the dining room with a tureen of thick vegetable soup. "We must celebrate Marguerite's arrival with that which warms all French people: good humor, pleasant weather, and delicious food," she said. Mother and daughter sat at the table set for the occasion with a white cloth and festive wine glasses. Marguerite looked sideways at her mother, glad that the descent into a sour mood was over.

A delicious wild mushrooms omelet followed the soup. "Henri Noyer picked those meadow mushrooms this morning on the way to the river." Florence told them. "You remember the field behind the Granger's farm, Marguerite?"

"Do I remember! We used to gather mushrooms with Pépé there—get up at dawn to make sure to find them before anybody else did. Sometimes we had to start walking with lanterns. I've rarely gathered mushrooms in California except for a few chanterelles when we lived in the Bay area. People are not as excited about wild mushrooms in America as the French and the Italians are. My husband was afraid of them."

After a light dessert of stewed apricots, and the mellow Rosé de Provence wine, the three women felt happy and close. No one wanted to complain about anything, no one wanted to break the peaceful atmosphere. Florence started to pick up dishes while Marguerite wheeled Claire out for an evening outing around the property.

The evening was balmy. The sun had begun to set behind the pine trees lining the back of the park. The mills had stopped their click and clack. Looking down at the soft tendrils of hair on the back of Claire's neck, Marguerite felt a great sense of love for her mother, so dependent now, the same woman whose strength had carried the family through so much, a woman nearing the end of her life.

"Mamie, we haven't talked about Germaine yet. How is my sister?" she asked as they headed back up the gravel path to the front door.

"Tomorrow, Marguerite. I'm suddenly tired and ready for bed."

Florence took over when they entered the hall and helped Claire with her evening routine. Marguerite climbed up to her room with a sense of fulfillment. The visit would be all right. Marguerite felt she wouldn't have to kick snakes any time soon.

MARGUERITE WOKE UP with a ray of sunshine on her face. She realized that she had slept for a long time and very likely missed breakfast. She automatically thought about Claire and what she would say, anticipating criticisms. She quickly put on her robe and walked down to the dining room. Florence was cleaning up, Claire was sitting next to the window with a magazine in her lap, and Marguerite's breakfast was on the table—toasted bread and jam, a croissant, and an empty cup.

"Good morning, Marguerite. It's good you slept so well," Florence said with a welcoming smile. "I'll bring your café au lait in a minute."

"Good morning, everybody. I feel rested. It's looks like a beautiful day."

"Good morning to you, dear," Claire replied, still looking carefully through her thick glasses at her magazine. "This article is fascinating; it's about snakes. They talk about the kind of vipers we have around here. Do you remember your dream about snakes when you were four, Marguerite? I had to keep you from crying after you woke up. You were so shaken."

"Yes, I do vaguely remember a few. We were warned so often about snakes when we were kids."

"But there was one dream in particular, though. It was amazing. Your sister was in it. Right?"

"Let me think a minute. Yes. Is this the one you mean? I was playing ball with Germaine and I had thrown the ball in the bushes. Germaine went to get it, disappearing into the bushes for so long I started crying and calling, 'Germaine, Germaine.' Finally, Germaine's arm stuck out of the thicket with a viper wrapped around it. I woke up in tears and very scared."

"We had to warn you kids about vipers because we wanted you to be careful."

"These things stay with you. Even Isabelle dreamed about a snake next to Justine's ermine stole. Try to explain that one. Maybe it's a family trait."

"Victor would tell you that it lies down in the basement with the spider webs. I don't want to look into all that stuff, although these days they say it has to do with psychology. I call it mumbo jumbo."

Florence brought a steaming pot of café au lait, and Marguerite spread jam on her toast with delight. "What a great breakfast. I'm famished. Right now, all I want is to enjoy my breakfast, Mamie, no more talks about snakes, please. I wouldn't mind catching up with Germaine. How is she?"

Mamie shrugged. "Germaine is well. She hasn't retired yet, still a pharmacist in the big city. It's sad. Her husband has Alzheimer's and her only son lives in Paris. She feels quite lonely. Don't you hear from her?"

Marguerite looked down at her hands. "Not really."

"Germaine is pretty distant, in every way. She comes to see me once in a while, but she's very involved with her job, her friends. She's always been a smart person but I think that makes her lonely. Can you see why I miss you and my granddaughter and I am upset you had to move away to America? I am stuck here, unable to travel, stuck with my memories, my regrets, and knowing that the end will be here soon."

"I'm surprised you don't see her more. You always held her up as an example for me, Mamie. Germaine was the one who always did things right. She went to college; she lived close by. I thought you felt like she was more what you wanted in a daughter, and I was more like Justine, the rebellious one because I left you and my country."

Claire remained silent and then said softly, "I hadn't thought of that. The comparison between Justine and my rebellious daughter makes some sense. Isabelle is looking for a family pattern between us. I guess that's what she means." Claire perked up. "Maybe you followed your heart, Marguerite, but your heart could have told you not to abandon your country and your family. Your heart was in the wrong place."

"Didn't you want some of those things in your own life, Mamie? Maybe you would've liked to go away, explore the world. Maybe you would've liked to wear beautiful clothes like Justine did. Sometimes the heart is undeniable. Look at Isabelle. I think she's doing this right now."

A tear fell down Mamie's lined cheek. Marguerite reached out and clasped her mother's hand. "I have an idea. Let's see if we can come to an understanding? Maybe you can let go of your resentment of my leaving you and my country, and I can forgive you for reminding me of this all my married life, including the fact that Justine's husband started the whole thing by enlisting my young husband in the resistance."

Mamie sniffled and gave a half-hearted nod.

"All this stuff is past and gone," Marguerite continued, "Life is made of these little twists of fate. Germaine led her life her way, I led mine my own way, and you did yours your way. Mamie, let's just enjoy what life is now. Can we? As a matter of fact, I can't wait another minute to eat this scrumptious toast." Marguerite took a huge bite and buttery crumbs scattered over the table and her shirt.

Claire grinned a little but remained silent while Marguerite enjoyed her bread dipped in the café au lait. She put her hand on her mouth, puckering her lips in a wondering way.

Marguerite took a final noisy sip of café and sat back. "I enjoyed this breakfast so much. Thank you. I wonder how is Isabelle doing now? Do you think she'll call? Mamie, you're so quiet. What's going on?"

"I think you got the last word, Marguerite."

Marguerite looked closely at Mamie's face. She didn't look bitter or angry. Marguerite could hear a shy humor in her tone. This was new. She liked this in her mother.

Claire continued, "We each did our lives our way and I better do mine before it's all over. I think Isabelle may have taught you something, too, or we wouldn't be talking like this, would we?"

"It feels very new."

"And the little detective is off on her own adventure as we speak."

They laughed gently at first, exchanged a glance, and then started laughing together so deeply and loudly that Florence rushed in to find out what was going on. When she saw that they were just caught in the throes of hilarity, she started laughing, too, until they all bent over and begged each other to stop.

XI

The Mirror

How does one begin to narrate a week of bliss? How can one translate into words the converging energies, the intuitive flow of each timeless moment, the melting of all tensions, and the comforting constant validation of each other? Isabelle felt closer to Philippe every day, and her sense of her own self started to change. It was as if she had entered a magic land, where their two divided selves became one, but, having tasted the wholeness of that magic place, she was able to effortlessly step back into her individual skin. It happened so naturally that she didn't notice when the transformations took place. Blending. Separating. Blending. Her knowledge of this new self was like awakening into a soft sunlit morning.

When did it materialize? Was it the day they walked around the rugged rocky terrain which surrounds the village, Philippe holding her hand tightly as they treaded the ancient grounds? They had imagined they were following the footsteps of prehistoric inhabitants, the Romans, Visigoths, and the 14th century marauders. They had climbed to the medieval hilltop town and walked a labyrinth of old streets, visited the Vasarely Museum to see the artist's large geometric paintings. Philippe revealed his vision in his art.

"I must capture light and space through color and textures."

"But Philippe, light? Is there really that kind of light in New York?"

"I am not looking for the light outside of myself. If I ever do, I will move to Provence or New Mexico. Right now I have to be where the museums, the art galleries, the other artists like me live. The light forms I visualize are in my mind's eye. It's like looking into a mirror to see myself."

Was it the day they had stayed in bed, all day, making love, drinking champagne, and listening to music? Philippe introduced Isabelle to one of his favorite pieces of flute music: the *Dance of The Blessed Spirits*, by Gluck. They had talked about Orpheus and Eurydice, and they let the enchanting melody transport them into another world. That evening, they had gone out to dinner to the Auberge de la Bartavelle and eaten Italian ravioli in a creamy chive sauce. They drank a 1982 Pomerol that had slipped down their throats like velvet, and then, they had come home to their cozy room knowing their bodies were magnificent instruments with which they could play heavenly music.

"Philippe, you are a Stradivarius." Isabelle whispered to her lover.

Was it the day they took a hike in the astonishing Canyon of Véroncle? They had wandered among the ruins of ancient dams, stone mills, and dried up riverbeds. They walked silently along the sheer rock walls of the canyon. The wilderness came alive in a lush meadow where butterflies floated over wildflowers and bird songs filled the air. They ate their picnic by one of the old ruined mills.

"This once-civilized place has returned to its primal wilderness. I like that. Nature is most elegant in its simplicity and its ruggedness."

Or was it, perhaps, their last day? Isabelle wanted to spend that evening together on a hill, watching the stars. They walked, holding hands, for a long time. When they arrived at the foot of the hill, they began to slowly climb the gentle grade, filling their lungs with the warm evening air. On top, the view glistened under the moonlight.

"I feel so small and so big at the same time. The universe is both inside and outside me."

"We have become transparent. I feel complete. Loved and loving."

"Philippe, you will always be with me. I know life will keep on flowing, but I will never lose this love. It's sacred."

He pulled her close. "We never lose what is sacred."

"Philippe, listen? I can hear our music playing in the stars, filling the air. I want to dance with you."

Philippe and Isabelle stood up and danced on top of the hill, swaying, holding each other close, and unleashing their soft moon shadows over the French countryside.

THE NEXT MORNING, they packed their bags quickly. They cleaned Pierre's place together, bought some wine and a dry flower arrangement for him. They left a little note: "Thank you, friend. It was a voyage to heaven."

Leaving town in the Peugeot, they took a last look at the village perched on the hill and turned into D2, heading for Avignon. They were lulled into a meditative state by the song of the cicadas and remained very quiet for a long time. Twenty kilometers north of Avignon, Philippe broke the silence.

"I was thinking of what you said last night, up on the hill, Isabelle—that you felt so small and so big at the same time. It just dawned on me that what you felt is what modern physics has been affirming all along."

"What do you mean?"

Philippe paused. "The whole is present in every part. You entered a state where you were aware of yourself as a part of the universe, of the whole, and yet the whole was present inside of yourself in its loving form. I've felt that way when I'm painting, but you said it so simply and clearly."

"We hold it all within us, don't we. I also think we each have both a personal destiny and one that's linked to the whole of humanity. Without diminishing our personal experience, it gives a different meaning to life. A much grander sense of spirit."

"I wonder, where the spirit of most people dwells today, Isabelle?"

"We're lucky to feel it so intensely. But for many—and for me for much of my life—I guess it's hidden in a forest of spider webs, as Victor would say, and we flail away trying to break it open."

"That's why we seek extreme experiences. Like climbing mountains, creating art, composing music."

"Making love."

"I almost forget the most important way to cross from dark to light: falling in love. That's transcending the self." They each smiled shyly and drove on, meditating on the exquisiteness of spirit.

Philippe softly stroked her arm and continued, "When the spider webs are too thick, looking for transcendence sometimes deadends in debased forms of high, like drugs, violence, or recreational sex. The players never find joy. If they only could taste the real thing."

"Dead souls make a mess of this earth. Do you think that this modern angst and chaos is a difficult but necessary step?"

"All I know is that I need to keep in touch with my center or I fall into chaos, too."

In Valence, they stopped for lunch at the same restaurant they had eaten at on their way to Provence. They took a walk in the park, sat on the same bench hugging each other. "We've made a quantum leap since we were here last," Philippe said, reaching his hands as far over his head as he could reach.

Isabelle took over the driving. Again, the two lovers remained silent for a long time, listening to the cicadas. There was one important issue Isabelle wasn't ready to tackle. By trying not to think of it, of course it crept in at every turn.

When they saw La Bâtie ahead, Philippe broke the silence. "We've done a beautiful job of living in the present, Isabelle, but there's something we can't avoid talking about."

She nodded. "I know."

"What exactly is our relationship?" His voice was deep and breaths separated his words.

"I'd like to close my eyes, to simply stay in this small space and talk like this, love like this. But I also know that we need to be free to be ourselves, to live as the spirit moves us, and do the work we're meant to do."

Their uncertainty filled the car. Isabelle felt so pressed by the contradiction of holding and letting go that she opened the window and leaned her head out into the wind and shouted, "I love you, Philippe. Be free! Be joyful!"

He slowed the car so he could watch her. Instantly the cicadas ceased their sweet humming. "The song of the cicadas has stopped and so has our magic journey."

Isabelle pulled back into the Peugeot with a deep contented laugh. "It's not over. It's in every cell of my being."

XII

Long Black Dresses

Philippe walked in with Isabelle when they arrived at the gate. He squeezed her hand and said, "I want to pay my respects to Marguerite and Claire."

Isabelle, still in the halo of their trip together, forgot to close the gate. She leaned against him briefly and grabbed Philippe's arm to stop him from walking farther, too.

"I didn't even call them when I was away," she said frowning.

"Don't worry, we were away for only a few days. They probably were very busy talking and catching up You've done a great job with Claire, she'll forgive you!"

Isabelle took a deep breath, let go of Philippe's arm, and started walking toward the door. She looked back at him in distress.

Philippe laughed at her worried face. "You act like Cinderella coming back from the ball."

This was what she loved about him: his ability to make her smile when she was slipping down. "Yes, but I have both shoes on and my prince is taking me home."

From the path, Isabelle saw Claire and Marguerite sitting in the garden under the linden tree, facing the mountains. "Coucou!"

The women turned their heads. "If it isn't our two prodigal love birds arriving… finally!" Claire said, staring at them with mock disapproval. "We were just talking about you and wondering if, or when, you would ever return? Well, you made it."

Blushing, Isabelle looked at Claire, then at her mother's grinning face. She realized she was being teased. She leaned down and hugged her. "Sorry I didn't call but there was no phone in Philippe's friend cabin and the next booth was quite a ways away from the place.

"Hello, ladies," Philippe interrupted with a large smile. "I wanted to tell you that I'm happy to see you both before I go back to my grandparents, who must be wondering where I am, too." Marguerite and Claire were silent. Philippe glanced nervously at his lover. "Isabelle and I had a wonderful trip to Provence. It's such a stunning part of France, an enchanting place. But now, if you don't mind, I'll leave and wish you three a great time together. Isabelle, I'll take you to the train station in La Tour du Pin next week. Okay? I'll keep the car a few more days. Enjoy your visit."

"Thanks, Philippe, and give my best to your grandparents. I'll see you next week." Isabelle looked forlornly at him, suddenly feeling torn from the cocoon of their new love.

"Nice seeing you, Philippe." Marguerite added with a grin. "The last time I saw you was way back, when you were in your twenties, I think. How time escapes us and how things change. Can you believe it?" She sighed. "Say hello to the family for me."

"Will do, Marguerite" Philippe replied backing away with a wave of his hand.

Isabelle stepped forward to walk Philippe to the gate, but she stopped in her tracks. This is the moment to begin being truly different in this relationship, she thought. Let him go. She sat quietly in a chair next to her family. Now, how would she start talking about what had happened? How would she explain how loving this man, this free and honest spirit had changed her life? How would she deal with these two formidable women who were so important to her?

Deciding the only way out of the awkward moment was to hit it straight on, she blurted out, "Well, I had quite a time. France has been good to me."

Claire and Marguerite quickly looked at each other then down, at a loss to respond to this declaration. The three remained silent for a while. Isabelle breathed deeply as if to inhale the last threads of her happiness. "Now, tell me what happened here. Did you two have a good visit?"

"We didn't fight this time, Isabelle. I think we decided to go into a sort of truce. I stopped talking about how bad I feel about you two leaving me for America. Marguerite forgives me for getting on her case for years about it. What do you think?" Claire proclaimed proudly, as if she had walked out of a long court battle.

"I'm so happy to hear this, Mamie. I was afraid the old story about Aunt Justine would come up and keep you both apart. For years now I've sensed Mom's love for Aunt Justine, and yet it was marred by your feelings about your sister. Mom would just shrug her shoulders when I would bring up the subject. Forgive me for bringing this again, Mamie, but it was hard for me to understand this since I wasn't in your shoes! I am relieved you can talk about it freely now."

"Well, little detective, I guess you found out a lot of stuff that I had never thought of before. You made me look at Justine differently, at her life, what I envied about her, you know, all the things we talked about and, to tell you the truth, I'm too old to fight anymore. I want to enjoy the rest of my life, whatever little there is." Claire relaxed back in her chair and closed her eyes as if she had put an end to a painful memory. The evening was slowly coming in as the sun started hiding behind the tall pine trees on the west. Two magpies flew by cackling. The air was balmy, giving a sweet tone to the situation.

Marguerite had been listening intently, "You know, I came back to mother's house expecting to fall into the same roles we played for years." She continued, shaking her head, "This new warmth feels like a balm." She rubbed her hands up and down her arms. "At the same time, there's something uncomfortable about it, like it's too good to be true perhaps?" She shook her head again and shrugged. "Well, whatever happened, it works for you, Isabelle." Marguerite sat up in her chair with an inquisitive look on her face. "So, when are you getting married?"

At first, Isabelle chuckled. "I can't believe this, Mom! The marriage strategy! Again! Actually, I was expecting this, sooner or later. It's another old story, right? You and Claire are one of a kind. The only thing you want for me is to get married. Will you ever trust that I know what I am doing?" She felt the heat rise in her face. "Okay, I'll calm down," she continued, taking a deep breath. "You two are still looking at me like a child. I know that you want the best for me, because you love me, but is marriage really the best thing for me right now?"

Claire put up her hands. "Hey, I didn't say it! By now, I trust that you'll do what's the best for you, Isabelle. Anyway you're probably too old to have kids at this point and marriage has to do mostly about family"

"That's true." Marguerite nodded, with a look of regret on her face, "But still, married would be nice. For some reason, I would have liked my only daughter to be married, and I would have done the mother, then the grandmother thing."

"You are like the somber women in long black dresses in my dream. You want me to marry… like in a storybook, Mom, with flower girls and the priest's benediction? And then the little ones running around in your antique shop?" Isabelle added taking her mother's hands in hers. "I guess I disappointed you?"

"Yes. I guess a little dream is a mother's prerogative for her daughter," Marguerite said with a heavy sigh.

"I am sorry Mom, but I may never get married." Isabelle paused. "Anyway, I'm very happy and feel good about myself and my life, right now." Isabelle continued, getting excited. "This trip has given me a new confidence in life. I found out how I relate to many of my women ancestors who had lost their husbands and I identified with their loss. Also, I saw how much I have in common with Aunt Justine, with my relationship to men, my spiritual life and all. You should see the beautiful things I found in the attic which belonged to her and that I will bring back!" Isabelle's enthusiasm was contagious as Mamie punctuated with head nodding and smiles.

"And then, Mamie has been great. We've discovered a lot of common ground between us. She must have told you."

"Yes, she did and it sounds as if you've unraveled a lot of the bits and pieces of your dream in the process. You did well, girl." Marguerite patted Isabelle's shoulder. "But, I see Florence coming out to get us for dinner. Are you hungry? I am."

"Of course I am," offered Mamie, sniffing the air, "can you smell what I smell?"

The three headed for the dining room, smacking their tongues in anticipation of another great soup, which they had been getting the scent of all along from the garden. It had to be leeks and potatoes, for sure.

Florence had made a delicious spinach quiche along with the soup, which they enjoyed with some chardonnay. Isabelle had quieted down and was now enjoying her dinner. The three women were quiet, as if they were taking a break from the conversation and reflecting while eating their dinner. They only murmured with pleasure as they sipped the wine.

"I'm tired but let's end the evening with a little music. Why don't you play *Autumn Leaves* for us, Marguerite?" Mamie asked pointing to the piano. "I like that song. Remember when it first came out in the forties and you kept singing it over and over? What were those words again that made you so sad? You used to cry at the end of the song!"

"*And the sea erases on the sand, the footsteps of the separated lovers,*" Marguerite slowly sang as she played the last bar.

"That is so sad, Mom. I can see why you cried. Splitting up is such a difficult thing, and the image is so strong! The sea erases the footsteps… "

"My sweet lover had died," Marguerite said softly. "I was so young and fragile! I thought I would never get over it. He was shot in the Resistance. It was horrible. I didn't even find out until a week after it happened and Justine let me know. She told me that he had died as a hero, but that didn't mean anything to me. I just wanted him back. I cried and cried for days. Mamie was mad at Justine, and she tried to keep things going, stoically, as always. She didn't realize how much I was affected." Marguerite was now

Isabelle's Dream

crying, holding her chin in her hand. "Life forces us to experience the worst of times when we are in the most vulnerable loving places." Marguerite continued, wiping tears from her eyes. Isabelle felt tears coming up, and Claire moved closer to her daughter, touching her gently. They remained silent for a while. "But it was a long time ago," Marguerite added, sniffing.

"I didn't realize all this, Mother," Isabelle whispered. "And you lost David, too."

"Yes, another loss!" Marguerite brushed the tears off her cheeks and waved her hand. "What's more important now is that your lover is alive, Isabelle, so let's all three sing something more joyful before we go to bed, something sweet, something which will make us feel that life is not that bad after all."

Claire broke into a French lullaby. "*Dodo, l'enfant do, l'enfant dormira bien vite, dodo, l'enfant do, l'enfant dormira bientôt.*" (Dodo, the child goes dodo, the child will sleep quickly, dodo, the child goes dodo, the child will sleep soon.)

"It feels like home again, like being a child. It actually makes me sleepy," Marguerite rose from her chair. "Good night, Mamie. Good night, Isabelle, sweet dreams."

Isabelle wiped one last tear off her mother's face. "Good night, dear."

Mamie rang the bell and Florence appeared with her quiet assurance to help her prepare for bed. "Sleep well you two," said Claire as she blew them kisses.

This is a true home, thought Isabelle as she nestled under her blanket, where happiness resides and sadness is not too far from it in the heart.

WHEN ISABELLE CAME DOWN for breakfast the next day, Claire was seated in her wheelchair by the window, reading a magazine, Marguerite was finishing her croissant dunked in the café au lait, and Florence carried Isabelle's breakfast to the table before being asked.

"You slept in for a long time, today, Isabelle. You must have been tired." Marguerite offered with a wink.

"Yes, I was. I slept like a baby. No dreams that I can remember, not even sweet ones unfortunately."

"I've almost finished this article. It was so long," Claire, added. "Good morning, Isabelle. Are you missing your Romèo?"

"Yes, I miss him. What were you reading, Mamie?"

"Mamie has been reading a long article about vipers." Marguerite puckered her lips in amusement. "We already talked about the snake in your dreams when you were away. This is a family obsession."

"The snake was dead, I remember, lying next to an ermine scarf, and I told Mom that it was a cotton mouth, a dangerous snake, but she poked it and it stood up fiercely. Something about Mom reviving an old dangerous wound about Justine's ermine scarf I found in the trunk in the attic."

"Too late, girl, we already covered this subject when you were gone. Mamie is now okay about Justine and her ermine scarf," Marguerite added hastily.

Isabelle looked nervously over at Claire wondering if this comment would revive her jealousy.

Mamie chuckled. "I was mad enough to cut the damn thing up at the time. Aren't dreams peculiar, anyway? How on earth could you have known about that?"

"It's because we're so close. My dream teacher helped me understand Mom's dream about her sister's disappearance into the bushes, and the snake wrapped around her arm. You know, the famous dream Mom had when she was four? Anyway, he says that Germaine became a pharmacist and the snake around the arm was a caduceus symbol, the symbol for healing and medicine according to Jungian ideas. That makes a lot of sense. That dream predicted the future and mine looked into the past. I guess dreams don't serve just one purpose."

"Still sounds strange," Marguerite said with a mouth full of croissant. "Snakes will never be my cup of tea."

"They're not always frightening, Mom. But you kicked the black cottonmouth. I think of that as a symbol of transformation."

"Transformation is exhausting," Claire added, closing her magazine. "It's hard to believe but that mumbo jumbo is starting to make sense to me, and it does seem to change things for the best." She stretched her neck and closed her eyes. "Today is my monthly appointment at the hairdresser, girls, so I'll leave you for while. Florence will drive me there and I'll see you for lunch." She looked from one to the other impishly. "Enjoy yourselves but don't talk about the fussy old lady. Now, transformation is the word and I hope Gertrude will do just that on my hair today: transform me into a beauty." Claire laughed from her belly and her daughter and granddaughter joined her.

Isabelle caught her breath and said, "You are absolutely gorgeous just as you are, Mamie."

Isabelle's Dream

AFTER CLAIRE LEFT, Isabelle turned to her mother and asked, "Shall we take a walk to the mill by the river?"

"Yes, it's a lovely path. It's lined with tall chestnut trees, and hazelnut bushes hang over the trail. They make a bright green tunnel I used to race through as a girl. Do you remember picking up snails after the rain, Isabelle? You must have been four or five years old, once, and you got so excited. You wanted to carry the basket but you kept screaming when one of the snails would start to slide out, 'Mom, it's slimy, it wants to slide up my arm. Eek! I hate it! Please, take it out, please.' But you wouldn't let us carry the basket. You always loved creatures, you were so curious about nature."

"I still am, Mom, "Isabelle replied laughing at the snail story. "This is such a sweet memory. I had forgotten about it."

Marguerite and Isabelle continued their walk to the mill, feeling the comforting sight of familiar surroundings and breathing in the moist air of the river. They came to the old *lavoir*, or wash house, now in ruins and overtaken by thorny weeds and shrubs.

"When I was a child, women still came here to wash their clothes. Listen. Can't you hear them laughing! I used to walk with Germaine to the farm behind the lavoir to get milk."

"Are you going to see your sister while you're here?"

"I probably should make a quick trip to Lyon for a couple days. I haven't seen Germaine in years. We don't communicate much. She is an intellectual, busy with her friends who are into medical research and heavy discussions. We don't have much in common, but we write each other once in a while about family matters. In a way, this visit might give me a chance to reconnect and talk about the past. Germaine was a little jealous of my sweet husband at the time, and I think that she felt guilty when he died but we never talked about all this. Maybe the time has come and she will be open to talking after all these years. I would like that," Marguerite said with a hopeful look on her face. "We might be friends again, like when we were kids! I miss that."

"It's only a two-hour trip from here to Lyon, Mom, Why don't you do it?"

"I guess I will. But I wouldn't be here when you leave."

"I'll spend my last days with Claire and I'll see you when we're back in the States. Enjoy your sister's visit, Mom. It has been so good that you came when you did, and I thank you for it. We've worked through a lot of feelings together."

Isabelle and Marguerite stopped on the side of the path and sat on cracked washboard laid across two rocks like a bench.

"I'm not going to ask more questions about Philippe. I can see that you are very much taken by him. You're old enough to know what you are doing. I appreciate how you paved the way to an understanding with Mamie. I've never felt so at ease with her. She's totally reconciled with Justine's memory now."

"It just took making a little crack in her shell and it all poured out. I think that Claire is getting close to letting go. She says funny asides about it being the end of her life. Although she looks as strong and perky as always, I noticed a lot of weak moments in her body. Her hand shakes sometimes, and she has a hard time seeing things. I felt sad to see her crying and talking about death, which she feels is just around the corner. At the same time, she's approaching it in a lucid and accepting way, with no regrets from her past. Getting that thing settled about Justine was big." Isabelle nudged Marguerite affectionately. "And also accepting all her gripes about us. She wants to live her last days in an easy frame of mind."

"I never thought I'd see this happen with my mother. I came here with all my defenses up, prepared to deal with her in the same old way. I didn't need them."

Marguerite and Isabelle sat in the sun by the river. The soothing sound of the water skipping over rocks spread its hopeful power of life into them. They sat wordlessly, savoring this special moment of acceptance.

MARGUERITE LEFT FOR LYON the following day. She kissed Isabelle on each cheek and said, "See you in California."

Mamie said, "Say hello to Germaine."

"*Au revoir*, Mamie. Save me a place at the table for next Monday."

XIII

Snakes

The next three days, Isabelle spent a lot of time with Claire. The old lady did not even attempt to hide her pain. She wept several times as she watched Isabelle prepare for her departure. She could not take her eyes off her granddaughter

"What am I going to do, now, Isabelle? I've grown so accustomed to having you here. Why does it has to be so painful to see you go?"

Isabelle pulled a chair next to her and reached for the gnarled hand of her grandmother. "I'm sad to leave you too, Mamie, but I've learned something very important from you: strength. Think about all that you've been through in your life. I know you'll be strong again, like you have always been." Isabelle grinned impishly, kissed Mamie's palm, and closed the old fingers around the kiss. "And remember, we've shared secrets together. My love will stay with you even when I am gone."

Isabelle packed Justine's grey dress, pink hat, and white lace shawl with her belongings. Inside of the hat, she folded the little paper napkin, on which Philippe had written, "I will always love you, Isabelle." He'd written it the day in Gordes they stayed in the room all day and made love and drank champagne. She stopped by the cemetery, once more, to tell Justine of her deep happiness. She gave a gift of lavender bath to Florence, who had been so very discreet and helpful and always loving towards Claire. Isabelle was finally ready to leave.

Claire and Isabelle had their last dinner together. Florence ate in the kitchen, that evening, having decided to let them have their privacy. With the meal, cooked for the special occasion, Florence had included a very old bottle of Bordeaux wine that she had pulled out from a dusty rack in the cellar. Grandmother and granddaughter sat quietly, savoring their delicate quenelles with a mushroom sauce.

"I will never see you again, Isabelle. I will die soon," Claire said, sniffing between two bites.

"You know we all die, Mamie," she answered softly. "It's a game of chance, just a matter of time. When that time comes for you, I'll be here if possible; if not I'll be in your heart, and at that time, close your eyes," Isabelle said, starting to cry, "and imagine that I'm rubbing your neck softly and talking to you. It will be a beautiful light."

Mamie sniffed and the corners of her mouth turned up. "Oh, that big white light at the end of the tunnel. More nonsense from Victor."

Seeing the resilient old woman bounce back to life, Isabelle sat back and took another sip of wine. "Anyway, Mamie, you're not going to die right this minute. Marguerite isn't back from Lyon yet."

The cuckoo clock began spitting out its two note call, piercing the atmosphere with such a ludicrous and incongruous sound that the two women broke into an uncontrollable fit of laughter.

Claire finally sucked in a deep gulp of air and held her hand to her chest "This stupid bird sounds tired." She did a perfect imitation of it.

"Mamie, you sound just like it. Cuckoo, cuckoo," Isabelle cackled. "And we go through life doing our little chirps, as regular as the cuckoo. Nature has the last laugh."

"Remember the evening I waited for you, Isabelle? And I was upset at you and I staged this dramatic reception. It was so funny." Claire continued laughing hysterically. "Yes, life is funny. All the things I did all along as if I had come out of the little tree house just on time to say: cuckoo… cuckooo… cuckoooooooo!"

"And what about the day we drank champagne with Florence, like three wicked little old ladies. Remember? It was hilarious."

"Isabelle, I can't stop. It's too funny."

"I wonder what Florence put in her cooking tonight?" Isabelle chuckled.

"Wine, lots of it."

"The wine was wonderful, that's for sure. It's so good to laugh with you, Mamie. I haven't laughed like this for a long time, not since I was a giggling little girl." Isabelle raised her glass.

"To life, to love, and to you, my granddaughter," Claire toasted. "And to all the cuckoos of the world," she added, drinking the last of France's finest magic potion.

After dinner, Isabelle gave Claire her last foot massage, telling her that she should perhaps ask Florence to take over after she left: "There is nothing like the human touch, Mamie, to make you feel good and heal you."

Claire yawned, emotionally tired, and Florence took her to bed after two juicy kisses on each cheek from Isabelle.

Isabelle got up early the next day. She finished packing a few items, put the room in order, and looked at the mountains through the east window.

Chambéry and Aiguebelette are somewhere in those mountains, she thought, remembering the scent of Philippe.

She put her cosmetic case in her purse, knowing that she had a long travel day ahead of her and that she would have to sleep in Paris, somewhere by the airport, in order to catch her late morning Air France flight to San Francisco the next day. "I wonder how Catharine spent her three weeks? I can't wait to hear her story!" she whispered to herself, now excited by the prospect of the travel ahead.

Claire was having breakfast when Isabelle came downstairs.

"Did you sleep well, Mamie?" Isabelle asked.

"Like a baby, Isabelle. I guess the wine must have helped a lot. We certainly had fun, last night, didn't we? I was just thinking of that when you came down."

The two women ate their breakfast quietly, each one knowing that the time had come to say goodbye.

After breakfast, Isabelle checked her watch. Philippe would be coming in a few minutes to take her to La Tour du Pin. She walked over to Claire and put her hand on her grandmother's forehead, stroking it gently. Her grandmother's chin trembled. When Claire attempted to speak, Isabelle put her index finger on her grandmother's lips and looked at her lovingly. Claire grabbed Isabelle's both hands, trying to keep her, just a little longer. Both women cried softly. Claire slowly released her grip, watching Isabelle walk out of her life, possibly forever.

Isabelle snatched her luggage and hugged Florence who was standing by the front door.

"Take good care of her. Claire will need you today. She's so sad, and so am I."

The faithful Peugeot was already at the gate. Its handsome chauffeur stepped out to put Isabelle's luggage on the back seat.

"I missed you, my sad love." Philippe kissed Isabelle on the neck. "It must have been difficult to say goodbye to your grandmother."

"I don't like goodbyes, Philippe, and the next one may be even more difficult."

"I don't like goodbyes either," he grinned, "but I'll run alongside the train—like we're in a movie—until I see your handkerchief disappear in the thick smoke."

"Oh Philippe, you are making me laugh. It's so good being with you again," Isabelle said, putting her head on Philippe's shoulder "I missed you too, my love."

They took the road to La Tour du Pin after getting down to the village. The church bells were ringing as they passed by the butcher's on the corner. It was Sunday and everything was closed. Isabelle remembered her feeling of excitement when she had arrived, a few weeks before. It had certainly developed far beyond what she could have ever imagined. She looked at Philippe; a man completely unknown to her three weeks ago had become a kind of soul mate.

"Let's trust the mystery of this."

"We still live here with our feet on the ground, and soon we'll be thrown back into our daily lives and their problems."

"I know, but I'm mostly simply seeing the exquisite things we've done together."

Philippe and Isabelle talked about the river, the Grande Chartreuse, making love, and watching the stars.

"Will you please say goodbye to Victor and Clémentine for me. I just couldn't leave Claire the last couple of days."

"Of course. My grandparents have been wonderful to me—the good fairies of my childhood. I owe them a lot."

Before getting to La Tour du Pin, Philippe stopped the car in a beautiful spot by the river. Away from people and traffic. They hugged tenderly, for a long time, their heads pressed together, and then they kissed, once more, gently closing their eyes.

The train from Lyon was already at the station when they got there.

"Remember Isabelle, just like a movie. You must get in now and play your part, and I'll play mine."

Isabelle took her luggage and climbed into a car in front of them. She walked to a compartment, put her luggage in the rack, and lowered the window. Philippe was there with all the love of the world in his hazel eyes. He threw Isabelle a kiss. As the train started rolling, he ran alongside extending his arm to the window, and handed Isabelle a large envelope.

"You look like Ingrid Bergman in Casablanca," he said, still running. "I love you, Isabelle." As the train gained speed, Philippe disappeared in the distance.

Isabelle pulled up the window, sat down, and looked at the surprise envelope. She wanted to open it but decided to treasure it for later, when she would be alone in Paris.

Isabelle closed her eyes. She cleared her mind of all thoughts and she went to that place, deep within herself, where silence soothes human emotions and love heals the crying soul. She realized she had not tried to hang on this man she so clearly loved.

Isabelle arrived in Paris in the afternoon. She took a room at the Holiday Inn, near the airport, looking forward to a restful evening before her long flight, the next day. She put her luggage down, threw the room key on the bed, and sat in a chair near the window to open Philippe's envelope.

There was a small painting inside. Isabelle looked at the strange arrangement of abstract shapes and colors, unable to translate these into a real thing or place or idea. She looked again, shutting off her mind's chatter, letting her soul feel the painting, and then, it dawned on her. Yes, the darkness and the light. The unusual composition spiraled to the top in a dancing wave—the reddish brown base and what looked like a lit sky. Philippe had painted their evening on the hill, in Gordes. He had imprinted their cosmic experience with the intuitive love of his insightful artistic soul. Isabelle held the painting to her heart, closing her eyes, overwhelmed by Philippe's thoughtfulness, overwhelmed by his love. Tears ran warmly on her face, erasing years of pain, years of groping in the dark, as she looked at Philippe's painting, dancing in his arms and hearing the music play on their magic hill.

Isabelle put Philippe's painting on the nightstand. Weary from the day's journey, she soon fell sound asleep.

SHE WAS SITTING IN A CAR *on the passenger seat. The driver was a man. He had a camera with him, and he looked delighted by the landscape. He was driving with one hand, shooting pictures with the other, and exclaiming his joy at the beauty all around. On the sun visor, in front of Isabelle, was a pocket, and there were two little snakes inside, sticking their upper bodies out and bobbing up and down as the car moved. At one point, the man stepped on the brakes and the two little snakes were thrown out on Isabelle. They started to crawl on her and inside of her clothes, slithering all over her chest and she said, "It tickles." She was not afraid at all. When the man stopped the car, farther on, the little snakes crawled out of Isabelle's clothes and she walked on with the man, holding hands, toward a hot tub...*

Madeleine Herrmann

ISABELLE, STILL SMILING, awoke and tried to decipher the meaning of her dream. She retraced each detail. She felt the language of her psychological studies flow. The dream, she knew, was about a balance between Animus, the masculine component of her psyche, and Anima, the feminine part. Her Animus was in control, driving the car, and taking photos of the inner landscape, the unconscious, excited by what *he* found. Anima was along for the ride and the baby snakes represented the deeper instinctive side, the sexuality, the awakening of the body by spirit guides. They walked together to the hot tub, the Mercurial alchemical bath, where transformation takes place.

Everything seemed clear to her now. She had come a long way since her first snake dream, filled only with elusive women, a negative mother energy, and a threatening snake. A transformation had happened inside of her, and Philippe had been a spirit helping to heal her.

Isabelle turned the light off and sank deep into her bed thinking: "I wonder what Catharine is going to say tomorrow?"

XIV

A Woman Named Isabelle

The sky was very overcast when Isabelle woke up the next morning, a repeat of their gloomy arrival weather. Isabelle ate a light continental breakfast in her room, expecting to be overfed and inactive on the plane. Lunch, dinner, and breakfast would be served during the eleven-hour flight back to San Francisco and the food would be very decent for airplane meals. Isabelle heard Clémentine's voice: "But, of course, you're flying on Air France!"

Isabelle took the hotel shuttle to Charles de Gaulle airport and walked to the Air France counter. On her way, she checked the monitor for flight departure times and was surprised to see that the San Francisco flight had been delayed one and a half hours. She checked her watch and sighed. "At least I'll have some company. Catharine should be here any time now."

Isabelle went through check-in and asked to have the seat next to her reserved for Catharine who was in the computer, and then she settled down close to the entrance and waited for her friend.

Half an hour went by. No Catharine. One hour, still no Catharine. Another half an hour. It was almost time for the original scheduled flight. "I wonder what's happened?" Isabelle asked in a low voice. "I know that Catharine has a tendency to be late, but this is becoming serious."

By eleven forty-five, Isabelle had given up on her friend and was going to proceed to the passport control and the duty free shops—when a hurricane blew in through the double doors, dragging her suitcases: It was Catharine looking anxious but fired up with energy. Isabelle watched her approach. She was dressed in a new fashionable red summer suit, she looked stunning with her blond hair and deep tan, and she seemed to have lost some weight. Isabelle got up, waved, and called to her.

Catharine dropped her bags with a thump. "Isabelle, thank god! Did we both miss the flight?" She gave her friend a hasty hug.

"Relax, the flight has been delayed. I got your seat assignment so you only need to go to the counter and check in."

Catharine brushed back a wisp of her hair and grabbed her bags again. They headed to the counter. "What luck. I thought I'd missed the flight for sure. I left Amsterdam early, at six, and my train arrived on time, but it took me ages to find a taxi, and then the traffic was so bad in Paris and on the freeway that we moved bumper to bumper for the whole trip. There had been an accident and only one of the freeway lanes was open. I am all stressed out. I really thought I would have had to wait for the next flight tomorrow."

Catharine started to calm down after she checked in and they walked to the gate area just in time to board.

Isabelle laughed at her exasperated friend. "Luck, the Universe, mysterious angels. Something really came through for you."

"More likely technical difficulties. I'm not so close to the great mysteries." She fastened her seat belt and leaned back with a big moan of relief. She turned to Isabelle with a spark in her eyes. "Anyway, here we are, on our way home. Remember when we left each other in Paris, four weeks ago? So much has happened since, I can't believe it."

"You can say that again!"

"I quit smoking."

That's grand. In Europe, no less, where everyone still smokes. It's good to see you so excited and happy. You look terrific, too!"

"I had the greatest vacation. I can't wait to tell you what happened."

"Let's tell our stories after we eat. They're going to serve lunch right this minute because our flight was delayed."

"I suppose I can wait," Catharine said, but then she grabbed Isabelle's arm and declared, "I had the most incredibly wonderful old fashioned fabulous affair."

"Aha, that's why you look so great, Catharine."

Catharine picked at her smoked salmon, her veal stew with tiny vegetables, and her camembert. Although she completely ignored the almond tart, she drank her small bottle of red Bordeaux. Lean Isabelle, on the other hand ate her whole lunch with great appetite.

After they finished their coffee and the stewardess had collected the empty cups, Isabelle turned to Catharine:

"So now, what was this most incredibly wonderful old-fashioned fabulous summer like?"

"At first I met my mother and we spent some time together. She has this great second story apartment by the canal, in Amsterdam. It's very pretty, lots of rugs, antiques, and a fireplace with those beautiful Delft blue tiles. Her place is very cozy and she has made a good life for herself. She has a white poodle named Mimi, she reads a lot and plays bridge three times a week with some regular friends. They come once to her place and she bakes cookies for them that day. The other times, she goes to their place. It really kept her busy this summer and that's good, because," Catharine raised her eyebrows at her friend, "as you know, we don't get along that well. It didn't take very long for us to start fighting, again. The same pattern as always. She tries to tell me what to do and I refuse, we fight, she sulks for a while and we make up. But, all in all, we did okay for two hardheaded women. We went to the Rijksmuseum together where I saw some incredible Vermeer paintings. The Woman In Blue Reading a Letter is the most beautiful thing I have ever seen, Isabelle. And The Little Street has such poetic beauty. I felt as excited as when we visited Giverny.

"The rest of the time, we went shopping, ate in Indonesian restaurants, and walked in the park but we also stayed home, watched some Dutch television, looked at old photographs and talked about life. Frankly, by the end of the second week, I was getting bored. We had gotten into a routine, and I hate routines, Isabelle." She grinned and closed her eyes. "But, believe it or not, it's thanks to this daily routine that I met Hans. Funny, isn't it?"

"Now I'm curious. What kind of a routine?"

"I walked Mimi, every morning, by the canal, and I noticed a good-looking man walking his cocker spaniel at about the same time. One day, the two dogs got into an argument, and we started talking to each other. He was a lawyer, in his early fifties, who had studied in the US at one time and was delighted to practice his English. His wife was staying with her sister for the summer, in the country, leaving the dog for him to take care of. After a few days of walking dogs together and getting acquainted, he offered to take me to Loosdrecht where he has a house on the lake and a sailboat. I simply couldn't refuse. Anyway, Hans had told me that he and his wife did not get along very well."

"That sounds familiar."

"I know, the typical line for married men. But I didn't want to get married to the guy, I was just looking for a wonderful affair which would give me a lift—and it sure did."

"Tell me about the lake."

"It was fabulous. He's got this great house on the shore with a sailboat docked right in the front of it. We went sailing, swimming, we made love in every imaginable position." Catharine whispered. "This guy is a sexual athlete, I'm telling you. We had so much fun. We laughed, we ate out in great restaurants, we had pillow fights, we cooked breakfast together in the nude—soft boiled eggs, smoked eel, fresh rolls, English tea."

"Food tastes so good when you're having great sex."

"I tell you, Isabelle, I had the time of my life. You can't imagine how beautiful it is driving through Holland's green grazing lands, the little towns, lots of steeples and some old windmills, flowers, lots of flowers. All together I spent ten days with Hans and each day was more fun than the other."

"Did you fall in love with him, Catharine?"

"I tried hard not to… maybe I fell a little. It's part of the playfulness of it." She paused, thought a minute, and then shrugged. "But truly, no, I'm not in love like that. We just had a great time and we separated without being torn apart. He might come to see me some day, when he visits his old Alma Mater in the States. In the meantime, I feel terrific. Reborn, renewed, rejuvenated, re-everything. The old Catharine in a new skin!"

"I bet you didn't visit any cemeteries while you were in Holland."

"You're teasing, rascal. But I confess, not one. I never thought about death once. Except perhaps when I left my mother. You never know what can happen when you live so far from each other."

"I had a hard time saying goodbye to Claire. I don't think I will ever see her again. She's almost ninety."

Isabelle and Catharine remained silent for a while. It was now six o'clock Paris time, and the plane soared over the Atlantic. Going west, they wouldn't see the next nightfall until they arrived in San Francisco.

"Imagine, Catharine, we'll be nine hours younger when we get to San Francisco."

"You are not going to tell me about Einstein now, are you?"

"I wouldn't know where to start."

"What's this beautiful old fashioned ring on your finger?" Catharine asked looking at Isabelle's left hand. "Did somebody special give it to you?"

"It belonged to my grandmother. My grandfather gave it to her and it has a lot of meaning for me." Isabelle gazed out the window.

"Hey, don't drift off yet. I told you my story, so now it's your turn." Catharine nudged her. "I want to hear all the details about your vacation. Did you retrace your family's past as you intended to do?"

"I did, Catharine. And my summer unfolded like a fairy tale."

"A fairy tale? I know you're a romantic, but I was hoping for something juicier than a fairy tale."

"This one is juicy. Are you ready?"

Catharine settled back into her seat, ready for anything. Isabelle remained silent for a few minutes, closing her eyes, and going back to the time when it all started. Then she gave Catharine an impish look and began:

"Once upon a time, there was a woman named Isabelle. She was a very good woman who had, somehow, been able to keep her child's soul very close to her heart. Her friends laughed at her and called her romantic, because they didn't understand her.

"Isabelle had been looking for true love, all of her life, but each one of her attempts at loving men had ended in disaster, leaving her without much self-confidence. One day she had a dream. The dream was so powerful that she thought there might be a clue to her misfortune in it, and wanting to unravel the mystery, she started on a journey to a foreign land.

"She arrived in a small village where her maternal grandmother lived, a very stiff old lady who seemed ravaged by a mysterious ailment. Her gaunt face made her look like she was wearing a mask. Her sour attitude was a mask, too. Isabelle was very sad to see her grandmother suffer; she wanted to help her, but the grandmother was not at all cooperative.

"The grandmother had a very nice maid. One day, the maid told Isabelle where the village shaman and his wife, the witch, lived. Isabelle went to their house, a cottage near the forest, to find out about her grandmother's past. There was a small cemetery in front of the cottage decorated with seashells, and the house was filled with characters out of all the storybooks. Isabelle was puzzled and somewhat scared. The shaman and his wife told her to look through the spider webs that hung in her basement. There she could find some clues to a spell put on her when she was born, they said. But, they also told her to look for the gifts that a good fairy had given her. 'Have courage,' said the shaman. 'You'll be fine,' said the witch.

"Back at grandmother's cottage, Isabelle started to rummage through the house, looking for clues to the past. She descended into the basement by searching through the past of her women ancestors and she discovered the curse of jealousy that had afflicted her grand aunt and her grandmother. Isabelle also found out what her own gifts were, by opening a trunk and a hat box in the attic and by reading some of her grand aunt's love letters.

"In the process, Isabelle faced her grandmother's secret. On a stormy night, after a terrible argument about the love letters, grandmother dropped her mask and cried. Because of their honesty, Isabelle and Grandmother became best friends. They lit a giant bonfire and burned some of the secret letters in a ritualistic fire together, saying goodbye to the old fears of the past and opening the way for a more generous and compassionate future.

"Isabelle was happy, she had found the answers to her misfortune and her good fortune, but she still needed to test out their powers.

"The test came the next day. A handsome prince appeared at her gate on a white powerful steed and he took Isabelle on a ride to a river where they played like children, then to a lake, where they kissed, made love on a bed of grass, and glided in a boat at sunset. The curse was starting to lift because she felt no expectations. She was happy to play in the moment.

"The handsome prince took Isabelle on a long trip, to a place where the land is warm and the insects sing about love all day. They had the most idyllic week there, they drank champagne, walked hand in hand, and Isabelle had many, many orgasms, even cosmic ones, especially one evening on a mountain top."

Catharine snickered. "And it was sooo spiritual!"

Isabelle nodded. "The handsome prince was a spiritual athlete, too. He taught Isabelle what bliss is really all about. When they said goodbye later, she was rid of her curse of fear and insecurity forever. She had become a whole person. Isabelle and the handsome prince had become loving soul mates who would live happily ever after… together or apart."

Isabelle stopped and looked at Catharine. "I don't know whether I should laugh or cry," Catharine said. She shook her head, frowning, sighing, and shaking her head some more.

"It's beautiful, Isabelle, really lovely. But you're speaking in riddles. I want to know more about this prince. What's his name?"

"Philippe. He's an artist and he changed my life."

The stewardess came down the aisle serving before-dinner drinks. She stopped in front of the two women. "What can I get you?"

"Champagne, by all means," Isabelle said.

"Champagne for me too," Catharine added.

The friends kept lifting their glasses while the Atlantic gently heaved below them. They toasted Hans. They toasted Philippe. They toasted their mothers and grandmothers and their amazing selves. Finally, Isabelle toasted the strange, revealing dream that had launched her journey into the unfathomable wonder called love.

About the Author

Madeleine Herrmann was born Madeleine Durand, in Lyon, France, on March 17, 1930. She and her family survived World War II in Nantes, which was bombed repeatedly and partly destroyed. In her teenage years after the war, Madeleine became a competitive athlete who won French National Track and Field titles. In 1949, she participated in the University World games in Budapest. While studying at the Ecole Normale Supérieure d'Education Physique in Paris, she received a Fulbright scholarship to study at the University of Iowa and came to the United States. There she met her husband, Fred Herrmann, a German student, gifted linguist, and violinist. They married and raised four children in California, building two houses together.

Madeleine pioneered physical fitness classes with music for women in the 1950s when women stayed at home, mostly as mothers, and had no exercise programs available to them. Madeleine enrolled in UC Berkeley and received her MA in 1962. After she graduated from UC Berkeley, she taught French at Del Valle High School for seven years until 1969, then at Diablo Valley College, in Pleasant Hill for another 23 years.

In 1983, Madeleine went back to college to study Transpersonal Psychology in the Master's program at JFK University in Orinda CA.

Fred Herrmann committed suicide unexpectedly in 1969 leaving Madeleine caring for their four children, between the ages of eleven and fourteen years old. Struggling with her husband's suicide, she searched assiduously for causes.

Her book of poetry, *L'envolée magique* (Editions Saint Germain des Prés) was published in France in 1986. She continued to write poetry as well as stories for both adults and children. In 2010, Madeleine published *Partita* (Plain View Press), a psychological mystery probing the reasons that drove Fred to end his life.

Following her consistent interest in the ways of the human psyche, Madeleine wrote *Isabelle's Dream*, which unravels the mystery behind a woman's dream about her family's emotional legacy.

Madeleine Herrmann has lived in Taos, New Mexico since 1992.

www.ingramcontent.com/pod-product-compliance
Lightning Source LLC
Chambersburg PA
CBHW052034070526
44584CB00016B/2038